# POMPEII

# TRAVEL

# GUIDE 2025

*Discover Ancient Wonders, Uncover Timeless Stories, and Navigate the Treasures of Italy's Lost City with Insightful Tips and Cultural Insights for an Unforgettable Journey*

**ANTHONY BOLDS**

ANTHONY BOLDS

# MAP OF POMPEII

## SCAN THE CODE TO ACCESS THE MAP

ANTHONY BOLDS

4 POMPEII TRAVEL GUIDE 2025

# ANTHONY BOLDS

## TABLE OF CONTENTS

# INTRODUCTION

When I stepped off the train in Pompeii, I felt like I had been transported back in time. The contemporary world appeared to melt away as the ancient city beckoned with hushed stories engraved in stone and ash. The cobblestone streets beneath my feet told stories of bustling markets, lively bars, and ordinary lives stuck in time. As I went among the relics of homes, stores, and temples, the sheer scope of the city's preservation astounded me.

The brilliant frescoes on the walls continue to flare with color, defying the passage of nearly two millennia. In the House of the Vettii, I marveled at the beautiful artwork depicting mythological scenarios, with each brushstroke having its own story. The imposing grandeur of Mount Vesuvius in the background acted as a striking reminder of the city's awful end, while also emphasizing the tenacity of human history buried beneath layers of ash.

The plaster casts of Pompeii's inhabitants struck me as particularly poignant. In their final moments, they contributed a truly personal aspect to the wreckage. It was impossible not to feel a connection, a deep pity for these folks, whose lives ended abruptly but continue to teach us so much about the past.

As the sun began to set, putting a golden glow over the ancient stones, I realized Pompeii is more than just a tourist destination; it is a voyage through time. It's a place where history is apparent, and every turn leads to a discovery. I left the city with not only memories of breathtaking vistas but also a deep appreciation for the fragility and everlasting spirit of human civilization.

# 10 REASONS WHY YOU SHOULD VISIT POMPEII

1. Learn about ancient history firsthand.

Pompeii provides an unparalleled opportunity to walk around a city locked in time. The volcanic eruption of Mount Vesuvius in 79 AD preserved buildings, artifacts, and even paintings, providing visitors with a direct view of ancient Roman life.

2. See Remarkable Archaeological Sites

The remains of Pompeii are among the best-preserved archaeological sites in the world. You can walk down ancient streets, enter houses, and witness everyday objects that tell stories from the past.

3. Discover the Culture of Ancient Rome

Visiting Pompeii provides an opportunity to learn about Roman culture, traditions, and daily activities. From the amphitheater to the baths, each site displays intriguing parts of ancient culture.

4. Admire Stunning Frescoes and Mosaics.

The city is home to stunning artworks, like as elaborate frescoes and intricate mosaics. These pieces shed light on the artistic achievements and aesthetic values of the time.

5. Educational Opportunities for All Ages.

Pompeii functions as an open-air museum, teaching tourists about history, archaeology, and geology. It's a rewarding experience for kids, instructors, and anybody curious about the ancient world.

6. Panoramic views of Mount Vesuvius

Standing in Pompeii, you can see Mount Vesuvius, the volcano responsible for the city's preservation. The vista is a striking reminder of nature's power and the events that have changed history.

7. Accessible location Near Naples

Pompeii is ideally placed near Naples, making it easy to reach by train or vehicle. It's an ideal day trip option for those exploring southern Italy.

8. Enjoy Italian cuisine and hospitality.

The area surrounding Pompeii is full of great Italian eateries and cafes. Visitors can sample local cuisine and enjoy the warm welcome of the Italian people.

9. Photographer's paradise.

The ruins offer limitless opportunities for photographers. Ancient structures, streets, and antiquities provide unique and interesting topics.

10. A Journey Back in Time

Visiting Pompeii is like stepping back in time. The city provides a fascinating and moving experience that ties you to the life of individuals who lived approximately two thousand years before.

# CHAPTER 1

## PLANNING YOUR ADVENTURE

## DECIDING WHEN TO GO

### Spring (March-May)

Spring offers pleasant weather and blossoming sceneries. Temperatures range from the mid-50s to the low 70s (°F), making it ideal for strolling and exploration. The crowds are lower than in the summer, making for a more relaxing visit.

### Summer (June-August)

Summer is the busiest tourist season in Pompeii. The temperature is scorching, frequently surpassing 85°F, and the place can get congested. If you don't mind the heat and want a lively atmosphere, now could be the time for you. Make careful to remain hydrated and use sunscreen.

### Autumn (September–November)

Autumn provides excellent weather, with temperatures ranging from the mid-60s to the upper 70s (°F). Summer crowds thin off, making it an ideal time for those looking for a more intimate encounter. The shifting leaves offer a unique appeal to the environment.

## Winter (December - February).

Winter is the off-season in Pompeii. The weather is cooler, averaging around 50°F, with a larger probability of rain. However, the location is far less busy, and lodging options may be more reasonable. Winter is a good option if you want a more personal encounter and don't mind bundling up.

## UNDERSTANDING LOCAL CLIMATE

During the summer months, temperatures can rise dramatically, providing long, bright days ideal for exploring ancient sites. The dry conditions this season suggest that outdoor activities are unlikely to be disrupted by rain. Visitors should protect themselves from the sun by dressing appropriately and staying hydrated.

Winter in Pompeii brings colder temperatures and more rainfall. This season reveals a different side of the region, with a more tranquil environment and fewer tourists. The warmer environment is great for people who want to avoid the heat while still visiting ancient places.

Spring and autumn are transitional months with mild temperatures and occasional rains. These seasons are frequently regarded as the most comfortable periods to visit, as the weather is good and the natural surroundings are particularly lively.

ANTHONY BOLDS

## TRAVEL DOCUMENTS AND VISAS

## Passport Requirements

All international visitors must have a valid passport to enter Italy. The passport should be valid for at least three months after your intended departure date from the Schengen area, which includes Italy. It is prudent to verify your passport's expiration date well in advance of your trip and renew it as needed.

## Visa requirements

Whether you need a visa depends on your country of citizenship.

1. Citizens of the European Union (EU), the European Economic Area (EEA), and Switzerland can enter Italy without a visa by presenting a valid national ID card or passport. These visitors are free to stay for as long as they choose.

2. People from the US, Canada, Australia, New Zealand, and several other nations: For brief visits of up to 90 days

during 180 days for business or tourism, a visa is not necessary. A valid passport is enough.

3. Prior to their arrival, citizens of other nations might need to get a Schengen visa. To find out if this applies to you, it is imperative that you speak with the Italian embassy or consulate in your home country.

## Applying for a Schengen visa

The Schengen visa allows up to 90 days of travel within the Schengen area over 180 days if one is required. The application procedure often includes:

1. Fill out a visa application form.

Provide a legitimate passport that has at least two blank pages.

2. Submit recent passport-sized pictures.

3. Provide documentation of travel arrangements, such as flight itinerary.

4. Providing documentation of accommodations, such as hotel reservations.

Obtaining travel insurance that includes medical emergencies with a minimum coverage of €30,000.

5. Demonstrating adequate financial resources to sustain your stay.

Processing times can vary, so apply well in advance of your scheduled trip.

## HEALTH AND SAFETY PRECAUTIONS

**Wear the appropriate footwear and clothing.**

The streets of Pompeii are lined with uneven cobblestones and ancient paths that might be difficult to maneuver. Wearing comfortable, durable shoes helps to avoid slips and trips. Because shade is scarce, particularly during the warmer months, consider wearing light, breathable clothing and a wide-brimmed hat to defend against the sun. Remember to apply sunscreen and bring a bottle of water to stay hydrated.

**Stay on marked paths.**

Certain places have been blocked to protect the site and visitors' safety. Always follow the authorized walkways and obey any obstacles or signs prohibiting entry. Deviating from the pathways can not only harm the fragile ruins but also endanger personal safety due to unstable buildings.

## Avoid touching artifacts or structures.

While it may be tempting to touch the antique walls and relics, oils and dirt from your hands can corrode these historical gems over time. Observing with your eyes, rather than your hands, helps to preserve Pompeii for future generations.

## Be mindful of personal belongings.

Pickpockets are more likely to strike in crowded settings. Keep your personal belongings secure, and consider wearing a money belt or storing valuables in your front pockets. Maintain awareness of your surroundings, particularly in congested areas such as entrances, exits, and popular attractions on the site.

## Use the Official Guides and Resources.

Using official guides or audio tours improves your comprehension of Pompeii's rich history and guarantees you get the right information. Guides are also aware of the safest paths and can point out any locations that may require particular caution.

## Check weather conditions.

Before you leave, check the weather forecast. Rain can slicken stone surfaces, increasing the risk of falling. If the weather prediction predicts rain, carry a waterproof jacket and traction shoes. In inclement weather, various portions of Pompeii may be restricted for safety concerns.

## Emergency Services.

Familiarize yourself with the archaeological site's emergency exits and services. Knowing where to go in an emergency can make a big difference.

# BUDGETING FOR YOUR TRIP

## Transportation

Begin by studying the most cost-effective ways to get to Pompeii. Booking flights to Italy in advance will help you get a better rate. Once in the nation, trains offer a dependable and inexpensive way to travel to Pompeii from places such as Rome and Naples. Buying tickets online ahead of time can occasionally result in discounts.

## Accommodation

Finding a location to stay within your budget is critical. Pompeii and the surrounding surroundings have a variety of lodging options, including hostels, bed and breakfasts, and budget hotels. Staying in neighboring towns may result in reduced pricing, so consider all of your alternatives before booking.

## Entrance fees

The archeological site requires a ticket purchase. Check the official website for current costs and see if there are any reductions available to you, such as student or senior rates. Sometimes combination tickets for many locations in the vicinity are a better deal.

## Meals and Dining

Eating out rapidly adds up. To save money, check for local restaurants that serve traditional dishes at moderate costs. Visiting markets to purchase fresh vegetables for snacks or simple dinners can also help you cut your food costs.

## Local Transportation

Walking is an economical way to see Pompeii and allows you to thoroughly appreciate the place. For longer distances, public transit is less expensive than taxis. Look into bus and train schedules to help you organize your trips more efficiently.

## Guided tours

Hiring a private guide can help you understand Pompeii better, but it may not be practical on a restricted budget. Alternatives include group excursions, which are typically less expensive, or using guidebooks and smartphone apps to supplement your self-guided tour.

## Souvenirs

Set a spending limit for mementos to prevent impulse buying. Local crafts and mementos are appealing, although costs vary significantly. Before making a purchase, compare shops to ensure you are receiving the greatest price.

## Travel Insurance

Including travel insurance in your budget is a sensible choice. It protects you from unforeseen events such as trip cancellations or medical problems, perhaps saving you money in the long term.

## Emergency Funds

Put away a portion of your funds for unanticipated costs. This could include everything from basic medical needs to unexpected events that you don't want to miss.

# SUSTAINABLE AND RESPONSIBLE TOURISM

It is impossible to overestimate the significance of responsible and sustainable tourism here. Visitors help ensure that this archeological gem is preserved for future generations by embracing activities that safeguard it.

Reducing the impact on the environment is a key component of sustainable tourism. Simple precautions, such as following designated routes, can help prevent damage to delicate remains. The place will stay clean and undisturbed if rubbish is disposed of appropriately. Reusable water bottles help with larger environmental initiatives by reducing plastic waste.

Getting involved with the local community is another aspect of responsible tourism. Employing local guides supports the local economy and adds genuine insights to the guest experience. Buying products from regional craftspeople promotes community economic viability in addition to providing one-of-a-kind mementos.

An essential element of ethical travel is education. Prior knowledge of Pompeii's background and cultural significance enhances enjoyment and promotes civil conduct while there. Everyone's safety and the preservation of the ruins are guaranteed when posted rules and regulations are followed.

Another crucial element is aiding conservation initiatives. Participation in volunteer activities or donations to preservation initiatives might have a noticeable impact. By supporting restoration efforts and continuing study, these initiatives contribute to the preservation of Pompeii's priceless legacy.

# CHAPTER 2

## GETTING THERE AND AROUND

## REACHING POMPEII

## BY AIR

The easiest way to get to the ancient Pompeii ruins is to fly into Naples International Airport (NAP), which is the nearest major airport to the location. Naples is a major entry point, with flights from many airlines connecting tourists from all over the world.

Airlines like United Airlines and Delta Air Lines offer flights to Naples from the US, usually with a stopover in a European city like Paris, Frankfurt, or London. Convenient connections are made possible by the routes that European carriers like British Airways, Lufthansa, and Air France offer to Naples.

Season, the time of year, the departure location, and the amount of advance ticketing all affect airfare costs. Flights to Naples from major U.S. cities typically cost between $700 and $1,200 round-trip. Getting cheaper prices can be achieved by being flexible with your vacation dates and planning.

Pompeii can be reached via a variety of modes of transportation after landing in Naples. The Curreri Viaggi bus service, which travels from the airport to Sorrento with a stop at Pompeii, is one effective way. The approximate cost of tickets for this service is €10. As an alternative, passengers can join the Circumvesuviana train line, which stops at Pompeii Scavi-Villa dei Misteri station, after taking the Alibus shuttle from the airport to Naples Central Station (Napoli Centrale). The total cost of this option is about €6.

Taxis and ride-sharing services are available at the airport for anyone who would rather go privately. A more direct and comfortable way to get to Pompeii is by cab, which usually costs between €80 and €100.

ANTHONY BOLDS

## BY TRAIN

### From Naples to Pompeii

The most direct route from Naples to Pompeii is via the Circumvesuviana train line, operated by Ente Autonomo Volturno (EAV). Trains depart from Napoli Porta Nolana or Napoli Garibaldi stations and arrive at Pompei Scavi - Villa dei Misteri station, located just a short walk from the main entrance of the ruins.

Frequency: Every 30 minutes

Duration: Approximately 35 minutes

Price: Around €2.80 one-way

Alternative Option: Trenitalia

Another option is the regional trains operated by Trenitalia. These trains depart from Napoli Centrale and arrive at the Pompei station in the modern town, which is about a 20-minute walk to the archaeological site.

Frequency: Less frequent than Circumvesuviana

Duration: Approximately 30-40 minutes

Price: Approximately €2.40 one-way

## From Rome to Pompeii

For travelers starting in Rome, high-speed trains operated by Italo or Trenitalia Frecciarossa connect Roma Termini station to Napoli Centrale.

Frequency: Multiple departures daily

Duration: About 1 hour 10 minutes

Price: Ranges from €20 to €40 one-way, depending on how early you book

## BY CAR

## Car Rental Options

Several well-known car rental companies operate throughout Italy:

1. Hertz: Offers a wide range of vehicles. Prices start at approximately €35 per day for a compact car.

2. Europcar: Provides various models with daily rates beginning around €30 for economy cars.

3. Avis: Known for reliable service, with small vehicles starting at about €33 per day.

4. Sixt: Features modern cars with prices starting from €32 per day.

Better availability and pricing can be guaranteed when reservations are made in advance, particularly during the busiest travel seasons.

## Driving Directions to Pompeii

1. From Rome: The trip is about 240 kilometers. Take the A1/E45 highway south toward Naples, then merge onto the A3 toward Salerno and follow signs to Pompeii. The drive typically takes around 2.5 hours.

2. From Naples: Pompeii is approximately 25 kilometers away. Drive south on the A3 highway toward Salerno and take the Pompeii exit. Typically, the trip takes half an hour.

Be prepared for toll roads along these routes. Tolls can vary but generally cost between €15 to €20 from Rome to Pompeii.

## Parking near the Archaeological Site

Several parking facilities are available close to the main entrance of Pompeii:

1. Pompeii Parking: Located near the site, charging about €10 per day.

2. Parking Zeus: Offers secure parking with daily fees of around €12.

3. Central Parking: Another option with rates of approximately €10 per day.

## Tips for Driving in Italy

1. Driver's License: An International Driving Permit is recommended alongside your home country license.

2. Traffic Rules: Observe local speed limits and road signs. Speed cameras are common.

3. Fuel Costs: Gasoline averages around €1.60 per liter, while diesel is slightly less expensive.

4. ZTL Zones: Be aware of Restricted Traffic Zones (Zona a Traffico Limitato) in certain areas to avoid fines.

## Advantages of Driving to Pompeii

1. Flexibility: Set your schedule without relying on public transportation.

2. Scenic Routes: Enjoy the Italian landscape and consider stops at attractions like the Amalfi Coast or Mount Vesuvius.

3. Convenience: Easily carry luggage and travel comfortably, especially if you're in a group.

## Cost Summary

1. Car Rental: €30-€35 per day for a compact or economy car.

2. Fuel: Approximately €30 for a round trip from Rome, less from Naples.

3. Tolls: Around €15-€20 one way from Rome; €2-€5 from Naples.

4. Parking: €10-€12 per day near the site.

## BY BUS

1. From Naples to Pompeii

SITA Sud Bus Company

Route: Naples to Pompeii

Departure Point: Naples Central Station (Piazza Garibaldi)

Frequency: Buses run approximately every 30 minutes

Duration: About 40 minutes

Price: Around €3 one-way

Travelers can catch the SITA Sud buses just outside the Naples Central Station. Tickets are available for purchase at the station's ticket booths or directly from the driver.

2. From Sorrento to Pompeii

EAV Bus Company

Route: Sorrento to Pompeii

Departure Point: Sorrento Bus Station (Via degli Aranci)

Frequency: Every 30 to 60 minutes

Duration: Approximately 50 minutes

Price: Approximately €2.80 one-way

The EAV buses offer a scenic route along the coast. Tickets can be bought at local tobacco shops (Tabacchi) or the bus station.

3. From Rome to Pompeii

Marozzi VT Bus Company

Route: Rome to Pompeii

Departure Point: Rome Tiburtina Bus Station

Frequency: Usually one daily departure in the morning

Duration: Roughly 3 hours

Price: About €20 one-way

For those starting from Rome, the Marozzi VT buses provide a direct connection to Pompeii. It's advisable to book tickets in advance due to limited daily services.

ANTHONY BOLDS

## Travel Tips

1. Advance Booking: Purchasing tickets ahead of time can secure your seat, especially during the busy tourist season.

2. Schedule Confirmation: Bus timetables may change on weekends and public holidays. Check the latest schedules on the official websites of the bus companies.

3. Ticket Validation: Remember to validate your ticket upon boarding to avoid fines.

4. Safety Precautions: Keep personal belongings secure and stay aware of your surroundings in crowded areas.

5. Guided Tours: Some bus companies offer package deals that include guided tours of Pompeii, which can enhance your visit.

# NAVIGATING THE CITY

# PUBLIC TRANSPORTATION

An easy and effective way to see Pompeii and the surrounding area is by public transit. The town itself is a great starting point for visitors because of its good connections to Naples and other neighboring sites. The Circumvesuviana line, which runs frequently between Naples, Pompeii, and Sorrento, is the most widely used form of public transportation.

From Naples Garibaldi Station, passengers can take the Circumvesuviana train straight to the Pompeii Scavi stop, which is the station nearest to the archaeological site. The ticket often costs around €3.60 one way, and the ride takes about 30 minutes. In addition to being reasonably priced, this alternative offers a rapid route to Pompeii's primary attractions.

It is useful to know that the Pompeii Scavi station is only a short stroll from the archeological park's main entrance for visitors who intend to see the ruins and other sights.

Easy-to-follow signs will direct tourists to the remains once they arrive.

The bus service that links different attractions in and around Pompeii is an additional mode of transportation. There are local bus services that go to neighboring locations like Vesuvius and Herculaneum. Bus tickets range in price from €1.30 to €2.50 for each ride, though this varies according to the destination. At stations, tobacco stores, or straight from the bus driver, tickets can be bought.

Use ride-hailing applications like Uber or taxi services if you want a little more flexibility. For shorter or late-night excursions, taxis are a convenient option because they are close to the train stations and popular tourist destinations. Remember that the starting price for a cab is about €5, and the cost will increase based on the distance and time of day. To prevent unpleasant surprises, it's a good idea to request an estimated cost before beginning your ride.

Renting a car could be a worthwhile choice for those who want to see more of the area. Naples is home to a large number of car rental firms, and owning a vehicle gives you the flexibility to explore less accessible locations at your speed. Be advised that parking in Pompeii might be scarce, particularly in the vicinity of popular tourist destinations. Typically, parking costs fall between €3 and €5 per hour.

## WALKING AND BIKING ROUTES

### Walking Routes

Walking through Pompeii is one of the most personal ways to experience its history. Visitors can walk down cobblestone streets, pass past historic residences, and see the remnants of temples, theaters, and markets. The self-guided walking pathways are straightforward, with well-marked signage describing major monuments and their historical background.

The archeological park's self-guided walk normally costs between $18 and $22 per person. This cost includes admission to the main attractions, allowing you to explore independently or follow suggested itineraries that lead you around the key regions of the site. Audio tours are available for an extra fee, typically approximately $10, and enhance the experience by providing lengthy narratives about each location.

Guided walking tours are another alternative for those looking for more detailed information. Professional guides provide tours lasting two to three hours, leading groups through the most iconic and noteworthy locations. These excursions typically cost $35 to $50 per person and offer historical insights and fascinating stories about Pompeii's past.

## Biking Routes

For those who like motorcycling, Pompeii's surroundings provide a variety of routes that showcase both the ancient and modern characteristics of the area. While riding is not permitted on the archeological site itself due to preservation regulations, the neighboring paths offer numerous possibilities to explore the region's natural beauty and other historical sites.

There are various rental shops near the archaeological park's entrance that provide bikes for $15 to $25 per day on average. Many rental firms provide maps and route recommendations customized to different ability levels. Some popular routes take bicycles through the nearby town of Boscoreale or along the picturesque roads surrounding Mount Vesuvius, which offer views of the volcano and the Bay of Naples.

Guided bike trips are also offered, and they typically run for two to four hours. These tours frequently include stops at vineyards, local farms, and vistas that provide panoramic views of the ocean and mountains. Guided bike excursions normally cost roughly $45 per person, which includes the rental charge and, in some cases, refreshments or a dinner highlighting local specialties.

**Tips for Your Visit**

The tourist center's materials make it simple to plan your walking or riding experience in Pompeii. Maps, water stations, and local guides are all available to help you make the most of your trip. Always wear comfortable shoes and carry a hat and sunscreen, as shade can be scarce in some areas of the site and adjacent trails.

## GUIDED TOURS AND PRIVATE GUIDES

To accommodate a range of interests and price ranges, Pompeii provides a selection of guided tours and private guide alternatives, guaranteeing that tourists may fully explore the ancient ruins. Here are some well-liked options to give you an idea of the experiences that are available and what to anticipate in terms of cost.

A great method to learn about Pompeii's history, architecture, and way of life before Mount Vesuvius' explosion is through guided excursions. Usually led by experienced, certified tour guides, these trips emphasize important locations like the Forum, the Amphitheater, and the Villa of the Mysteries while offering interesting commentary. Group tours typically run for two to three hours and provide participants the opportunity to see important areas of the site. Depending on the length of time and the size of the group, these group trips typically cost between $40 and $60 per person.

Private tours are provided for those seeking a more individualized experience. These professionals provide specialized excursions that are tailored to individual interests, such as Roman art, ancient engineering, or daily living in Pompeii. Private tours give you the freedom to explore the ruins' lesser-known parts, go at your speed, and ask any questions you may have. Depending on the length of the tour and any extras like early admission or special access to areas that are forbidden, the cost of a private guide can range from $150 to $300 or more.

Specialized excursions are also offered, such as those that concentrate on the effects of the volcanic eruption, the cuisine and beverages of ancient Pompeii, or the artwork and murals that adorn the walls of its structures. These specialized tours, which provide an in-depth exploration of specific facets of Pompeian culture, typically have a predetermined focus. Although the cost of these specialty trips can vary, small-group experiences usually start at $80 per person.

It is feasible to combine Pompeii with neighboring sites like Herculaneum or Mount Vesuvius for those seeking a more immersive experience. Some operators provide full-day packages that cover lunch, transportation, and multiple site visits with a guide. Depending on what is included, these all-inclusive cruises might cost anywhere from $100 to $200 per person.

Due to limited availability for both group and private trips, it is advised to make reservations in advance, particularly during the busiest travel times. In order to help guests maximize their time without having to wait in lengthy lines, many suppliers also give skip-the-line services. Some trips provide pick-up services from neighboring cities like Naples or Sorrento for added convenience.

# CHAPTER 3

## THE RICH HISTORY OF POMPEII

## LIFE BEFORE THE ERUPTION

Before the eruption, Pompeii was a thriving hub of trade, art, and daily activities, painting a vivid image of Roman life. The city was alive with activity, from bustling markets full of dealers and craftsmen to beautiful homes decorated with elaborate paintings. The streets were lined with businesses offering everything from fresh fruit to luxury textiles, demonstrating the affluence and diversity of its citizens.

Pompeii's residents lived a sophisticated lifestyle, absorbing Rome's cultural influences while keeping their distinct local flavor. Public baths were gathering places where people not only washed but also socialized, exchanging the latest news and gossip. The amphitheater, a staple of the city's entertainment scene, staged gladiator games and performances, attracting people from all walks of life. This emphasis on leisure and community activities demonstrated the significance of social bonds in Pompeian society.

Religious life was strongly ingrained in Pompeii, with temples dedicated to various gods and goddesses scattered around the city. Citizens took part in rituals and festivals to worship their deities with offerings, prayers, and festivities that brought the community together. These practices represented Pompeiians' deep spiritual connection to their surroundings and the deity.

At the same time, the city was an architectural marvel, with buildings and public spaces that exemplified a combination of utilitarian design and artistic beauty. The Forum, the center of public life, was where politics, trade, and religion converged. Grand homes, covered with mosaics and murals, depicted the everyday lives and aspirations of Pompeii's wealthy elite, whereas simpler residences presented a humbler, but equally rich, story of the city's working classes.

Pompeii's economy relied heavily on the agricultural lands surrounding the city. Farms and vineyards supplied olive oil, wine, and other necessary products that not only fed the local inhabitants but also circulated throughout the region. The lush soil, fed by prior volcanic activity, makes this region one of the most prolific in the Roman world.

Every area of Pompeii reflected a flourishing, integrated community. Pompeii before the eruption was a site where life thrived, from the murmur of traders in the marketplaces to the craftsmanship shown in homes and public structures, and every instant offered an opportunity to experience the richness of Roman culture.

## THE CATASTROPHE OF 79 AD

The Catastrophe of 79 AD was a watershed point in history that permanently altered the environment and the lives of the people of Pompeii. When Mount Vesuvius erupted, it unleashed an enormous force that buried the entire city in volcanic ash and pumice. Exploring Pompeii today provides a look into this dramatic moment in which time appears to have paused. As visitors wander through the historic streets, they can see the remnants of buildings, homes, and temples that were once bustling with life. This conserved site depicts the daily lives, culture, and tragedies of a community caught off guard by natural disasters.

The eruption began with a column of smoke and ash reaching miles into the sky, obscuring the sun and causing confusion. The ash began to fall, blanketing the city as residents fled and others sought refuge. The weight of the piling ash caused roofs to fall, and finally, a flood of hot gas and molten rock descended the mountain, burying everything in its path. The individuals and animals involved in this catastrophe were immediately frozen in time. The casts of their remains, kept in the positions in which they were discovered, are some of the most poignant reminders of the disaster's magnitude.

Visitors to Pompeii today can wander through ancient markets, public baths, and theaters that were once bustling with activity. Detailed mosaics, frescoes, and even graffiti still adorn the walls, providing insight into the creativity, humor, and daily lives of those who lived there. The Forum, once the center of social and commercial activity, remains a symbol of the ruins. Visitors can see the magnificence of Roman architecture and learn about how public areas were created for commerce, political gatherings, and religious activities.

Pompeii's well-preserved ruins illustrate the lives of its inhabitants, from the wealthy villas, complete with atriums and private gardens, to the smaller, simpler residences. Stepping into these locations reveals how diverse the population was, with people of all classes and trades contributing to the city's vibrant environment. The ancient amphitheater is another example of Pompeii's robust culture since it hosted events like as gladiator fights and performances to entertain inhabitants.

Today, Pompeii is more than simply a historical place; it is also an opportunity to reflect on the power of nature and the fleeting nature of human undertakings. Each turn exposes a new story a mural showing a period in a merchant's life, a roadway leading to a bakery still stocked with ancient loaves of bread or a villa that once hosted grand celebrations. The eruption's impact, while terrible, has allowed for a remarkable amount of preservation, allowing modern-day visitors to connect with the past in an authentic and meaningful way.

## REDISCOVERY AND ARCHAEOLOGICAL FINDS

The centuries-long tale of Pompeii's rediscovery illuminates an ancient city that has been locked in time. A thorough record of Roman life was preserved when Pompeii was blanketed in layers of volcanic ash and pumice after Mount Vesuvius' eruption in 79 AD. Despite its destructive effects, this natural calamity preserved the city's buildings, artifacts, and even human impressions, enabling future generations to discover a thriving world that was nearly two thousand years ago.

Although the ruins of the city were discovered in the 16th century, official excavations did not start until 1748. At that time, archaeologists were amazed at how well-preserved structures, frescoes, and commonplace items were. From public baths and theaters to villas and marketplaces, every discovery provided insight into everyday Roman life. The painstaking paintings and frescoes that depict mythological themes, everyday activities, and symbolic imagery provide a striking window into the past and demonstrate the aesthetic and cultural ideals that the Pompeiian people held dear.

As technology develops, these archeological endeavors have persisted into the modern era and have grown more complex. Entire communities, complete with elaborate mosaics and the remains of enormous courtyards, have been unearthed during recent excavations. Researchers have discovered private homes with personal possessions, public areas with statuary, and kitchens with cooking implements still in use. Pompeii is a remarkable example of ancient Roman home architecture and urban planning because of these discoveries.

When you visit Pompeii today, you may see the ruins of houses and stores, stroll down avenues where chariots once traveled, and take in the magnificence of the temples and forums that were the center of public life. From the colorful graffiti that covers the walls to the remarkably lifelike plaster casts of the city's residents, immortalized in their last moments, every inch of the site tells a tale.

We learn more about Pompeian society and the Roman Empire overall thanks to the archaeologists' continuous efforts to uncover fresh parts of the city. The dynamic social fabric of ancient periods is shown by excavations that uncover not just magnificent monuments but also the daily lives of common people. These findings provide a thorough picture of the city's prosperity and hardships, giving visitors a rare chance to see history meticulously restored, piece by piece.

Pompeii serves as a potent reminder of history's tenacity and the lessons that might be learned from the past.

**ANTHONY BOLDS**

# PRESERVATION EFFORTS AND MODERN-DAY POMPEII

Preservation efforts in Pompeii have been instrumental in transforming the ancient site from a buried ruin into a place where history comes to life. After the catastrophic eruption of Mount Vesuvius in 79 AD, the city was sealed under volcanic ash, preserving homes, temples, and artifacts remarkably well. Today, this preservation allows us to witness ancient Roman life in a way that few other places can offer.

Modern efforts focus on maintaining this delicate balance between exposure and conservation. Archaeologists and scientists work together to ensure that the structures and artifacts uncovered are protected against weathering and damage. This involves using advanced technologies like laser scanning and 3D modeling to document every detail, ensuring that a digital record exists, even if the physical site faces future challenges.

One significant initiative is the Great Pompeii Project, which has seen extensive funding and international collaboration aimed at stabilizing buildings, repairing damaged frescoes, and implementing protective measures to reduce erosion and decay. Specialists carefully clean and restore wall paintings, using non-invasive techniques to preserve original colors and details. Floors are reinforced, and ancient drainage systems are restored to manage the impact of water on fragile structures.

Modern-day Pompeii is not just an archaeological site but a place of active learning and discovery. Visitors can observe these preservation efforts in action and appreciate the work that goes into maintaining the integrity of this historic city. The ongoing conservation projects ensure that this UNESCO World Heritage site remains a valuable resource for both educational and cultural enrichment.

# CHAPTER 4

## TOP EXPERIENCES IN POMPEII

## MUST-SEE HISTORICAL SITES

## THE FORUM

The Forum in Pompeii is a must-see attraction that provides a view into the heart of the ancient city. As the heart of public life, the Forum used to host social, political, and religious events. Walking among its remains, you'll see a remarkable collection of temples, market booths, and public structures that reflect the city's former liveliness. The remnants of constructions like as the Temple of Apollo and the Basilica disclose much about Pompeii's people's lives, worship, and commerce practices.

Entry to the Forum is included in the Pompeii general entry ticket, which normally costs roughly €16 for adults. Prices are reduced to around €2 for EU citizens aged 18 to 25. Visitors under 18 and teachers accompanying groups are frequently granted free admission. Purchasing tickets online ahead of time is recommended because it allows you to avoid lines and make the most of your visit. Consider combining your admission with on-site guided tours, which cost between €10 and €20 per person and provide professional insights into the Forum's history.

Private guides provide in-depth excursions tailored to your interests, with prices ranging from €50 to €100 depending on time and party size. Hiring a private guide not only broadens your comprehension of the ancient ruins but also allows you to explore lesser-known features and hidden sections of the Forum, resulting in a deeper, more complete experience.

## THE AMPHITHEATER

Pompeii's amphitheater commemorates the city's history and the Roman passion for entertainment. This ancient structure, one of the world's oldest surviving amphitheaters, provides a look into the past when gladiators fought and people assembled for public shows. Built in 70 BCE, it predates Rome's Colosseum and is a fascinating piece of architectural and cultural history.

Visitors to the amphitheater can tour the oval arena, where warriors once stood, and walk through the hallways where inhabitants once applauded, immersing themselves in the colorful life of ancient Pompeii. The building's stone tiers provide a clear view of the arena below, revealing how the Romans meticulously planned their amphitheaters to handle vast audiences while giving visibility to all visitors.

Understanding how to navigate entry charges and visiting suggestions can improve the experience for modern tourists.

Tickets to the Pompeii archeological site, which include entry to the amphitheater, normally cost roughly €16 for adults. Children under the age of 18 frequently receive free entrance, and EU nationals aged 18-25 may be eligible for reduced charges. It is best to check current pricing online before planning a visit, as ticket prices can fluctuate or vary depending on the season or special events.

## Visiting Tips:

1. Arrive Early: Visiting in the morning, especially during peak tourist season, can help avoid crowds and provide a more peaceful experience while you explore the amphitheater and adjacent ruins.

2. Wear Comfortable Shoes: The pathways and ancient stone steps can be uneven, so strong, comfortable footwear is required to navigate the region securely.

3. Take a Guided Tour: An experienced guide can bring the amphitheater's history to life, providing insights into its construction, use, and significance in Pompeii. Group tours typically cost between €20 and €30 per person, although private guides might cost between €60 and €100, delivering a more personalized experience.

4. Stay Hydrated: Summers in Pompeii may be scorching, and because most of the amphitheater and surrounding remains are exposed, it's essential to bring water. There are also water faucets on the premises where guests can replenish their bottles.

5. Photography: The amphitheater is a great place to take photos, so bring your camera or smartphone. Early morning and late afternoon are the best times to photograph the ancient stone constructions against the backdrop of the ruins.

## THE VILLA OF THE MYSTERIES

The Villa of the Mysteries in Pompeii is one of the most amazing and well-preserved archeological sites, providing insight into the ancient Roman world. This house, located just outside the city walls, was originally a wealthy residence, and its well-preserved frescoes attest to its historical and artistic significance. The name derives from the vibrant wall paintings located inside, which are thought to depict an initiation process into the religion of Dionysus, the deity of wine and ecstasy.

When you come, you'll see a variety of chambers decorated with exquisite murals that highlight the creativity of the time. These frescoes, rich in color and richness, depict events from life, mythology, and spiritual rituals. As you wander through, you may sense a link to the past, envisioning how these chambers formerly served as venues for both daily life and religious ceremonies. The pictures on the walls have attracted researchers and visitors alike, prompting concerns about the villa's function and the individuals who lived there.

To get the most out of your visit, arrive early. The site can get crowded, especially during peak tourist seasons, so scheduling your visit in the morning offers a more serene experience. The Villa of the Mysteries is included in Pompeii's standard entrance ticket, which costs approximately 18 euros for adults. Students and young visitors are eligible for discounts, while EU citizens under the age of 18 can enter for free. It's best to buy tickets online to avoid long lineups, and guided tours are offered for an extra cost, providing deeper insights into the site's history.

A few practical recommendations for your visit: wear comfortable shoes as the terrain is rough, and bring drink, especially during the warmer months. The home is located a short distance from Pompeii's main center, so expect a brief walk. Many visitors find it useful to bring a guidebook or download an audio commentary for context, as this helps them appreciate the villa's rich tales and creativity.

For photographers, the Villa of the Mysteries provides numerous opportunities to capture the spectacular frescoes and architectural elements. Remember that flash photography is prohibited to protect the delicate colors, so make use of natural light during your visit.

## THE HOUSE OF THE FAUN

The House of the Faun is one of Pompeii's most opulent and historically significant mansions, providing insight into the richness and refinement of ancient Roman society. This amazing edifice, which covers a whole city block, offers insight into Roman art, architecture, and daily life. Visitors can visit its well-preserved chambers, gardens, and mosaics, which depict the luxury lifestyle of its original inhabitants.

The House of the Faun, built in the second century BCE, was a lavish display of wealth. Its name is derived from the bronze statue of a dancing faun situated in the atrium. This statue, which represents joy and freedom, remains a symbol of the estate's splendor. The villa is intended to optimize light and space, demonstrating Roman architectural expertise. Wander through its two peristyles open courtyards encircled by columns which served as a pleasant retreat for the dwellers. These grounds, formerly thriving with plants and fountains, exude a sense of serenity.

The mosaics at the House of the Faun are its most striking feature. Among these is the famous "Alexander Mosaic," which depicts the conflict between Alexander the Great and Persia's King Darius III. Though the original is conserved at the National Archaeological Museum in Naples, a duplicate in its historical context allows visitors to understand how art was used to represent authority and distinction.

When visiting the House of the Faun, it's useful to know basic information regarding entry fees and advice to have a pleasant experience. Admission to Pompeii provides admission to all open sites, and prices normally range from €16 for a standard ticket to roughly €30 for a combined ticket that includes other nearby attractions like as Herculaneum. For those who want to save time and learn more, guided tours are available at an extra cost. Private guides, who provide a more personalized experience, often start around €50 per person, depending on the group size and length of the tour.

To avoid crowds, arrive early in the morning or late in the afternoon, particularly during the summer months when Pompeii is busiest. Wearing appropriate shoes and bringing water are also recommended, as the place is enormous and discovering its attractions may take several hours.

ANTHONY BOLDS

# THE GARDEN OF THE FUGITIVES

The Garden of the Fugitives in Pompeii provides a compelling look into the life of those who once called the ancient city home and the tragic conclusion to which they met. The castings of thirteen people who sought to flee the eruption of Mount Vesuvius in the year 79 AD can be found in this region of Pompeii, which is situated in the southern portion of the city. These figures, preserved in their final moments, serve as a disturbing reminder of the unexpected calamity that swept the city.

Walking through the garden, visitors may see the plaster casts, which reveal the details of the victims' attire, postures, and expressions. It's a chance to observe history in a concrete sense, linking modern visitors with a story fixed in time. The layout of the garden, with its rows of ancient grapevines, mirrors how this site was formerly used for farming, providing another degree of authenticity to the experience.

It's necessary to check the current entry costs and availability. The entrance cost to Pompeii's archeological site, which includes access to the Garden of the Fugitives, is roughly €16 for people. Discounts are often given to children, students, and seniors. Purchasing tickets online in advance can save time, especially during busy tourist seasons when lineups can be long.

To get the most out of the visit, wearing comfortable shoes is essential, as the ancient walkways might be uneven. It's also helpful to carry water, especially during the warmer months, as shaded spots may be limited. Hiring a private guide or attending a small group tour can offer in-depth insights into the history and significance of the site, enriching the whole experience. These tours normally range in price from €20 to €50 per person, depending on the group size and duration.

## HIDDEN GEMS AND INSIDER TIPS

## LESSER-KNOWN VILLAS

The Villa of the Mysteries is a must-see. It stands notable because of its well-preserved frescoes, depicting mystery initiation procedures. Located on the outskirts of Pompeii's city center, this home delivers a unique experience sans the regular throng. The paintings here, painted in vibrant red and detailed figures, give a window into the mysteries and rituals of Roman society. The entry charge is normally included with a standard Pompeii ticket, which costs roughly $19 for adults. Consider arriving early in the morning or later in the afternoon to experience a quieter ambiance.

Another buried treasure is the House of the Vettii. While smaller in scale, this estate boasts beautiful frescoes and original mosaics that speak volumes about the wealth and taste of its past occupants. The detailed wall paintings represent scenes from mythology, giving a gallery-like ambiance. It's a wonderful destination for people inquisitive about Roman art outside the iconic houses.

Access is also covered with the normal entry ticket to Pompeii. To make the most of your visit, look into attending a guided tour, which may cost roughly $35 per person, adding dimension to the experience.

The House of the Faun is another choice. It's one of the largest and most luxurious residences in Pompeii, however, it typically doesn't draw the same attention as other places. This villa's great design and mosaic flooring, especially the famed Alexander Mosaic, exhibit the artistic talents of the time. General entry to Pompeii covers access to this villa, and guided trips start at roughly $30 per person. Opt for an afternoon time when the light highlights the mosaic intricacies.

The Villa of Diomedes is another lesser-visited building worth exploring. Located just outside Pompeii's city walls, this home offers a unique perspective with its extensive gardens and terraces overlooking the Bay of Naples. The villa's serene surroundings and spacious layout make it a pleasant stop. Entry is part of the main ticket, but special guided tours are available starting from

$40, delivering in-depth explanations of the villa's architecture and historical significance.

## ANCIENT FRESCOES AND MOSAICS

Directly painted onto damp plaster walls, the frescoes provide a window into the fashions and hues of the ancient Roman world. Villas like the Villa of the Mysteries, where scenes of rites are depicted in exquisite detail, are home to some of the most amazing sculptures. Other noteworthy frescoes can be seen at the House of the Tragic Poet and the House of the Vettii, where the artwork uses colorful characters and symbolic significance to tell stories through composition.

Conversely, mosaics were frequently employed to adorn floors and occasionally walls, forming intricate designs or portraying portraits, animals, and gladiatorial combat. A spectacular battle scene between King Darius III and Alexander the Great is shown in the Alexander Mosaic, a masterwork found in the House of the Faun. The great degree of talent and craftsmanship displayed by the Pompeiian artisans is evident in these elaborate sculptures.

Knowing the admission costs and the best ways to view these historical artifacts is useful when making travel plans. Pompeii's normal admission price is about €18 per person, however, pensioners and students with proper identification can receive discounts.

Consider scheduling a guided tour, which normally costs between €15 and €25 on top of the entrance charge, for a more thorough experience. Expert commentary and context are provided by guided tours, which enhance comprehension of the significance of each piece of art.

Entry is free on the first Sunday of the month, but because it's a popular day, it's best to arrive early to avoid long lineups. Another piece of advice is to bring water and suitable walking shoes because the site is large and frequently takes many hours to tour completely. The most important frescoes and mosaics are simpler to find thanks to the maps that are offered at the entrance.

# THE TEMPLE OF APOLLO

An outstanding example of ancient Roman architecture and religion is the Temple of Apollo in Pompeii. Situated close to the Forum, it functioned as a place of worship and an essential component of the city's religious and social life. It is among the earliest buildings in Pompeii, having been built as early as the sixth century BC.

Its Corinthian columns, which still exude grandeur despite time and Mount Vesuvius' eruption, are open for admiration by tourists. The significance of Apollo in the Pompeians' daily existence is emphasized by the altar and the bronze statue of the god, which is oriented to catch sunlight.

Taking the time to study the architectural intricacies while touring the site provides a better understanding of the advanced design methods used at the time. The fusion of Roman and Greek architecture demonstrates the cross-cultural interactions that shaped the city's development. Apollo's significance in the life of the ancient residents is demonstrated by the surrounding columns, some of which are still surviving, which frame a view that links the past and present.

Arriving early in the morning or late in the afternoon will help you make the most of your stay by avoiding the heat and crowds, especially in the summer. There are uneven stone paths in the area, so comfortable shoes are a must. Because there aren't many places to find shade, it can also be more fun to bring a hat and a bottle of water.

Adult standard admission to Pompeii costs about €19, which includes admission to the Temple of Apollo. EU nationals between the ages of 18 and 25 and children under the age of 18 are eligible for free or discounted admission. To avoid the lines, it is advised to buy tickets online in advance.

# INTERACTIVE EXHIBITS AND VIRTUAL REALITY EXPERIENCES

Modern technology brings the past to life, giving us a better grasp of how this once-thriving culture worked. Visitors can walk through restored marketplaces, residences, and public spaces, learning about daily life, culture, and the catastrophic eruption that preserved the city for millennia.

Virtual reality stations are strategically situated to take tourists through the various eras of Pompeii's history. These thrilling experiences recreate what the city looked like before Mount Vesuvius erupted, allowing visitors to explore the streets and buildings as they once stood. The technology offers a vivid and educative vision of the past, making it simpler to understand the severity of the calamity and its impact on the people of Pompeii.

Interactive exhibitions supplement these virtual experiences by providing hands-on learning opportunities. Visitors can interact with digital displays, which contain rich information about the city's architecture, artifacts, and social norms. The exhibitions frequently include touchscreens that let visitors explore individual places, such as ancient homes, shops, or temples, providing an in-depth look at how life in Pompeii was arranged. These exhibitions help us better appreciate Pompeii's social organization, trade, and artistic achievements.

Some exhibits focus on the eruption itself, with animated animations depicting how the volcano erupted. Visitors can follow the chronology of events and learn about the geological processes that shaped the region thanks to these exhibits. It's a wonderful way to interact with the site's history since you can view Pompeii's destruction and preservation as if you were there.

These activities are appropriate for visitors of all ages, ensuring that everyone feels connected to Pompeii's past. With interactive and virtual activities becoming an intrinsic part of the site, exploring the ruins becomes an active journey through time, making the visit both educational and memorable.

# CHAPTER 5

## EXPLORING THE ARCHAEOLOGICAL PARK SUGGESTED WALKING ROUTES

Exploring the ruins of a city that has been frozen in time is an amazing opportunity provided by the Archaeological Park of Pompeii. Before Mount Vesuvius erupted in 79 AD, Roman life was reflected in this expansive site. The daily activities of a bustling Roman city are revealed to visitors as they meander through historic streets and view the remains of residences, businesses, temples, and public areas.

Maps and information guides are available at Porta Marina, the main gate, where you can begin your visit. The design of the park makes it possible to explore important locations, like the Forum, which serves as Pompeii's commerce and political hub. From there, you can explore the Basilica, the Temple of Jupiter, and other neighboring ruins that were previously used for important public purposes.

As one moves through Pompeii, one may see a variety of Roman architectural and design elements, from modest dwellings to lavish villas. Large and opulent, the House of the Faun is renowned for its expansive courtyards and elaborate mosaics. Further on, the Villa of the Mysteries enthralls with its remarkably intact frescoes, providing an insight into prehistoric customs and beliefs.

Consider starting in Porta Marina and walking in the direction of the Forum for a recommended walking route. Before heading to the Stabian Baths, where the remnants of public bathing facilities depict the social life of Pompeii's residents, spend some time touring the nearby temples and basilicas. Proceed to the House of the Vettii, which is renowned for its beautiful courtyard and artwork.

Walk toward the Amphitheater, one of the oldest of its kind, where gladiatorial contests formerly delighted the populace, to discover more of the city's attractions. The Grand Palaestra, a facility for sports training, is located nearby. In addition to covering the main attractions, this route gives you the freedom to explore further if you so want.

Carefully organizing your trip enables you to see Pompeii's vast site in its entirety. Given the expanse of the park and the potential for weather exposure, it is advised to wear comfortable shoes, stay hydrated, and apply sunscreen. Depending on the length and level of depth of the tour, hiring a private guide is another choice. These professionals provide enlightening excursions that enhance your knowledge of Pompeii's history and architecture, and their fees often range from $50 to $100 per person.

## UNDERSTANDING ROMAN ARCHITECTURE

The architecture of Pompeii reveals a great deal about the everyday lives, social institutions, and aesthetic values of its inhabitants. Shops, residences, temples, and bathhouses litter the streets, each having a unique story to tell. Ancient Roman household life is revealed through the well-preserved remnants of the dwellings, or domus. You may see elements that were the main attraction of Roman residences, such as atriums, which are open courtyards frequently embellished with statues and gardens. The social element of Roman architecture was emphasized by the fact that these areas were used for both entertaining and private family purposes.

The city's civic and spiritual life is reflected in its temples and public structures. One architectural wonder that blends Greek and Roman features is the Temple of Apollo. The altars and columns are intended to catch the eye, displaying the majesty that was essential to religious buildings. These temples were constructed to dazzle both locals and tourists, serving as both places of prayer and status and power symbols.

The public baths were built with the well-being of the people as a top priority for Roman architects. Roman civilization placed a high value on social events and leisure, as evidenced by the Stabian Baths. Hypocausts, an early type of central heating that allowed hot air to travel beneath the flooring, were among the sophisticated heating systems included in these elaborately built baths.

These buildings' meticulous attention to detail demonstrates how the Romans were able to blend architectural beauty with mechanical mastery.

You may see ruins of the governmental structures, marketplaces, and temples that once constituted the center of Pompeii's public life as you stroll through the Forum, the city's main square. The Forum's architecture demonstrates the Romans' focus on open, public areas where social interactions, politics, and trade took place. Roman city design was structured to create surroundings that were both aesthetically beautiful and useful, and this is reflected in the layout.

Intricate theaters like the Large Theater, which can hold thousands of people, are another marvel of Pompeii. Because of the exceptional acoustics provided by the semi-circular structure, speeches and performances could be heard by everyone in the audience. These theaters' survival demonstrates how important entertainment and public meetings were to Roman culture.

The ornamental features that ornamented structures also exhibit the influence of Roman architecture. Ancient mosaics and frescoes, which frequently portrayed themes from mythology or everyday life, were essential to boosting the aesthetic appeal of residences and public areas. These decorative elements give the architecture depth and demonstrate how Roman aesthetics was characterized by a fusion of practicality and creative expression.

Every building in Pompeii, from the smallest store to the largest temple, adds to the story of a city that was meticulously constructed with an awareness of both beauty and functionality. As a testimony to the Roman architectural legacy, this amazing fusion of engineering and creativity gives visitors today an opportunity to engage with the past in a real and significant way.

## ARTIFACTS AND THEIR STORIES

Walking around Pompeii, visitors come across relics of a lively society. Clay pots, kitchen equipment, and other domestic goods depict the city's daily routines and culinary customs. These artifacts depict a lively household life in which food preparation and social gatherings were important for family and community. The tools and utensils, meticulously constructed and kept, reflect the skills and crafts passed down through centuries.

Mosaics and frescoes on walls and floors are among the most fascinating discoveries. These art styles not only demonstrate the skill and inventiveness of Pompeii's artists, but they also tell a story about mythology, daily life, and cultural values.

For example, the House of the Faun features a detailed mosaic representing the Battle of Issus, demonstrating an interest in historical and mythical themes. Each fragment conveys a tale about what was cherished and appreciated, offering insights into the cultural attitude of the time.

# ANTHONY BOLDS

Statues and sculptures dispersed around Pompeii serve as mute witnesses to the city's history. Some feature gods and goddesses, symbolizing the spiritual beliefs of its population, while others display important personalities, demonstrating society's appreciation for its leaders and influences. These sculptures frequently depict fashion, hairstyles, and societal standing, bringing to life the people who previously walked the city streets.

Even more personal are the casts of victims found in the rubble. When archaeologists poured plaster over the gaps left by decaying bodies, they created breathtakingly detailed images of Pompeii's residents, frozen in their last moments. These actors present moving stories that remind us of the abrupt calamity and the humanity behind the debris. Their looks and stances indicate a city caught off guard, where regular life has been disrupted by a single catastrophic occurrence.

Coins, jewels, and other luxury artifacts demonstrate the thriving trade and business in Pompeii. The city's position made it a center of economic activity, and these artifacts demonstrate the wealth amassed by its citizens. Examining the artistry of these products, which range from highly carved coins to delicate bracelets, provides insight into the city's economic and creative life.

Pompeii's amphorae, which originally held olive oil, wine, and other necessities, demonstrate the city's involvement in larger commerce networks around the Mediterranean. These storage boats, stamped with signs indicating origin and trade routes, demonstrate the city's connection to distant places and involvement in commerce. Historians and archaeologists have used these items to reconstruct trade patterns and economic exchanges that helped Pompeii thrive.

## PHOTOGRAPHY TIPS AND REGULATIONS

First and foremost, you must comprehend the lighting. Early mornings and late afternoons are ideal times to shoot the ruins since the natural light is gentler and more flattering. This timing also avoids the intense midday light, which can cast shadows and impair the exquisite details of paintings and stone carvings. Arriving early not only provides better lighting but also allows you to avoid heavy crowds, making it simpler to capture unobstructed images of the historic streets and structures.

Remember that Pompeii's beauty is in the details. Look beyond the huge structures and concentrate on tiny details, such as the mosaic patterns or the texture of the walls that have weathered ages. These close-up photos can highlight historical workmanship and provide a more in-depth look at ancient Roman life. Using a macro lens might help you capture these fine details with clarity.

Be aware of the photography regulations in force. To ensure the archeological site's integrity, certain restrictions must be followed. Tripods and selfie sticks are frequently prohibited to avoid inadvertent damage and to make routes clear for other guests. It is recommended that you check for revisions to these restrictions before visiting, as they are subject to change. Handheld cameras and smartphones are often permitted, making them useful tools for documenting your trip.

ANTHONY BOLDS

When photographing frescoes and old artworks, avoid using flash. Over time, flash photography can damage these priceless objects by losing their colors. Instead, rely on natural light and, if necessary, increase your camera's ISO. This allows you to capture the splendor of antique art while avoiding harm.

Please respect the privacy of other visitors. Pompeii is a renowned tourist spot that draws visitors from all over the world, so be considerate when taking photos. Focus on the ruins and landscapes rather than other tourists in your photographs, unless they contribute to the scene's ambiance and are not the major topic.

Take the time to plan out your photos in advance. Familiarizing yourself with Pompeii's layout and important attractions, such as the Temple of Apollo or the House of the Faun, will help you focus your photographs. This planning guarantees that you catch all of the highlights as well as the hidden treasures, resulting in a diversified and thorough photo collection.

**ANTHONY BOLDS**

By adhering to the site's laws and approaching photography deliberately, you can build a collection of photos that not only chronicle your visit but also preserve Pompeii's timeless wonder for future generations.

# CHAPTER 6

## TAILORED ITINERARIES

## ONE-DAY HIGHLIGHTS TOUR

To benefit from lower temps and more peaceful routes, start your day early. The main sections are easily accessible from the Porta Marina entrance, so start there. Proceed in the direction of the Forum, which served as Pompeii's political and social center. With the city's temples and marketplaces encircling this main area, you'll get a sense of how people conduct their daily lives.

Next, visit one of the city's most significant religious locations, the Temple of Apollo, which is close by. Roman religious customs are revealed through the statues and columns. One of the most impressive homes, the House of the Faun, is only a short stroll away. The richness and artistic talent of the era are demonstrated by the intricate mosaics and the well-known statue of the dancing faun.

Following your exploration of these locations, proceed to the Baths of the Forum, which provide an insight into

Roman bathing customs and the elaborate architecture of these public areas. You may also view historic stores, bakeries, and residences that give you a true idea of everyday Roman life by strolling down the main streets, such as Via dell'Abbondanza.

It's a good idea to stop and relax about lunchtime in one of the neighboring cafes or sheltered spots outside the grounds. After that, go to the Garden of the Fugitives, where victims' plaster casts from the eruption capture a moving moment in time.

As the day goes on, don't forget to stop by the Amphitheater, which is among the oldest and best-preserved in the world. When you stand in the arena, you can practically picture the gladiator fights and huge meetings that used to occur there.

Travel to the Villa of the Mysteries, which is situated outside the city, for the last stop on your one-day tour. The remarkably well-preserved frescoes here provide a profound glimpse into the religious and magical rituals that some of the locals engaged in.

**ANTHONY BOLDS**

## TWO-DAY IN-DEPTH EXPLORATION

Day 1: Unveiling the Heart of Pompeii

On the first day, concentrate on the main places that depict daily life in ancient Pompeii. Begin at the Forum, the center of public activity, where you'll see the ruins of municipal buildings and temples that once served as political, religious, and commercial hubs. The Temple of Apollo is a must-see, demonstrating the influence of Greek architecture. Spend time learning about the layout and the significance of the remaining sculptures and columns.

Next, head to the House of the Faun, a magnificent example of Pompeii's residential architecture. Admire its vast layout, private courtyards, and well-preserved mosaics. The 'Alexander Mosaic' is a well-known piece that provides insight into the period's craftsmanship. Walk into the neighboring Baths of Stabian, an ancient bathing complex that demonstrates how the Romans prioritized cleanliness and relaxation.

Take a midday stop at one of the eateries near the site's entrance for a modest supper, keeping the pace easy but rewarding. In the afternoon, take a short walk from the center to the Villa of the Mysteries. This villa is well-known for its complex murals depicting initiation rites, which provide insight into Roman society's mysteries and rituals.

Day 2: Exploring Pompeii's Hidden Corners

The second day delves deeper into Pompeii's residential and commercial activities. Begin with a visit to the House of the Vettii, a well-preserved home decorated with brilliant murals depicting gods and mythology. This property belonged to two affluent freedmen, and its rooms reflect the luxury and prestige symbols that the owners prized.

Continue to the ancient amphitheater, which represents Roman entertainment culture. This arena, which predates the Colosseum, featured gladiatorial conflicts and public shows. Walking amid the ruins, picture the lively mood of the spectators who previously packed the seats.

**ANTHONY BOLDS**

After that, visit the Garden of the Fugitives, which features plaster casts of persons captured in the eruption's final minutes. This melancholy encounter serves as a poignant reminder of the tragic events that happened here. The preserved emotions and postures offer a personal and moving dimension to Pompeii's narrative.

Finish your day by visiting the bakery ruins, where you will find old ovens and milling machinery. It's an interesting stop that highlights the city's business life as well as its residents' daily activities. Consider how ancient and current food preparation and commerce activities are related.

## FAMILY-FRIENDLY ADVENTURES

Families can take part in kid-friendly interactive tours that combine exploration and storytelling. These tours frequently incorporate entertaining games like treasure hunts, in which children are given maps and hints to find secret locations and learn about Pompeii's history in an interesting and developmentally appropriate way. Children can experience an adventure where they can pretend to be young archaeologists or ancient Romans when they visit the Villa of the Mysteries or the Forum.

Pompeii has adopted contemporary innovations to improve the experiences of tourists who are interested in technology. Families can view reproductions of historic neighborhoods and structures through virtual reality excursions. Children can see what Pompeii looked like before the catastrophe thanks to these interactive experiences that bring the ruins to life. For younger audiences, the archeological park's interactive displays, which include touchscreens and 3D models, add excitement to learning about the past.

Families can also opt for shorter walking paths that highlight kid-friendly attractions, such as the thermal spas that functioned as gathering places or the bakeries where historic bread was baked. These shorter routes provide a sense of Pompeii's history while also being ideal for small children's energy levels.

Renting a family audio guide that offers interesting information and stories appropriate for all ages is another enjoyable way to explore. Families can explore in comfort with these guides' customizable tour pace options, which ensure that no one is left out of the fascinating history.

Families may easily take a break and eat together while thinking back on their excursions thanks to the picnic sites that are close to the entrance. Traveling with children is made convenient by the well-indicated restrooms and other amenities.

Pompeii is the ideal family vacation spot because of its capacity to enthrall tourists of all ages. You can make enduring memories and cultivate a love of history in young minds by organizing a trip that combines exploration, narrative, and interactive activities.

## FOR THE HISTORY ENTHUSIAST

### Start at the Forum.

Begin your day in the heart of Pompeii, the Forum. This ancient plaza served as the city's political, economic, and religious core. The wide field, surrounded by remnants of temples and public buildings, is an excellent starting place for learning about Pompeians' daily lives. Walking through the Forum provides insights regarding the city's administrative power and influence in nearby regions. Stop visiting the Basilica and the Temple of Apollo to admire their architectural masterpieces and imagine the thriving society that once existed there.

### Explore the streets of Pompeii.

As you stroll down Via dell'Abbondanza, one of Pompeii's main streets, take note of the arrangement of stores, houses, and public baths. This walkway demonstrates how Pompeii residents balance work, recreation, and community. Look for old graffiti carved into walls, which gives voice to residents who lived approximately two thousand years ago. These streets also provide glimpses into the socioeconomic structure, with stark contrasts between the modest residences of commoners and the lavish villas of the wealthy.

## Enter the House of the Faun.

The House of the Faun is one of Pompeii's most outstanding houses. This sprawling mansion is a marvel of Roman construction, providing an exceptional glimpse into the wealth and creativity treasured by the city's elite. Admire the beautiful mosaics, which include a famous representation of Alexander the Great's fight, and imagine the splendor of Roman household life. This stop not only displays the aesthetic sensibilities of the time but also gives a feeling of the affluence that existed before the city's tragic demise.

## Visit the amphitheater.

The Pompeii Amphitheater is the world's oldest stone structure and a must-see for any history buff. Consider the energy and excitement as citizens came to witness gladiatorial conflicts and public spectacles. This well-preserved monument, with its huge arena, provides a tangible link to ancient entertainment and its cultural value in the town. Spending time here offers us a better grasp of the social thread that binds individuals together in ancient Pompeii.

## Discover the Villa of Mysteries.

A short stroll from the city center takes you to the Villa of Mysteries, a villa known for its magnificent frescoes. These paintings, with their vibrant colors and rich design, reflect what are thought to be hidden rituals or ceremonies. The estate encourages guests to interpret the scenes and investigate the potential implications of the ceremonies represented. It's a must-see for everyone interested in the mystery and spirituality of ancient Rome.

## Conclude in the Garden of the Fugitives.

End your historical excursion at the Garden of the Fugitives, a somber reminder of the eruption's aftermath. This website maintains the casts of those who attempted to flee the horrific incident, capturing their last moments. Reflecting on these characters creates a poignant connection to the past, reminding viewers of the human tales underlying the archeological remains. This location not only enriches the historical narrative but also stimulates reflection on the fragility of life and the legacy of Pompeii's residents.

## ROMANTIC ESCAPES

Pompeii is a great place for couples looking for a romantic adventure as well as history buffs. With its cobblestone streets and secret gardens, this historic city's ageless beauty creates the perfect atmosphere for an unforgettable visit. With the hues of the sky combining with the ancient stones, strolling hand in hand amid the ruins as the sun sets over Mount Vesuvius may create a wonderful scene.

Consider scheduling a private guided tour for a more personal experience. This lets you and your significant other take your time exploring the city's more sedate areas. You can follow an informed guide to magical locations such as the Villa of the Mysteries, where the vibrant murals depict tales of celebration and love. The ruins of Roman fountains and sculptures provide a peaceful backdrop in the lesser-known courtyards and gardens, where you may also find peace.

One way to enhance your romantic day could be to have dinner at a nearby winery with a sunset view of Pompeii. Wine tastings and meals based on old recipes are served at many of these local enterprises, making them a great way to end your trip. Pompeii provides couples with an amazing trip through time, full of chances to make treasured moments together, thanks to its picturesque surroundings and ancient atmosphere.

# CHAPTER 7

## BEYOND POMPEII

## MOUNT VESUVIUS EXCURSIONS

## HIKING TRAILS

The "Gran Cono" trail is the primary route to the crater. This well-traveled path has a moderate degree of difficulty and is roughly 2.4 miles (3.9 km) round trip. It begins in the parking lot of Vesuvius National Park, which is accessible from neighboring cities like Naples and Pompeii by vehicle or shuttle.

Although there are some steep parts of the hike, most people find it to be feasible, and it usually takes one to one and a half hours to finish. The well-kept trail leads to the crater rim, where visitors may get a close-up look at the volcanic features, and is marked with signage.

Because temperatures can fluctuate rapidly, particularly at higher elevations, visitors are advised to wear comfortable clothing, sturdy hiking shoes, and a lightweight jacket. Because there isn't much shade along the walk, sun protection is also advised. For individuals who require extra assistance, the park offers walking sticks, which are particularly useful in the steeper areas.

Whether you opt for a guided tour or a self-directed trek will affect the excursion's cost. They charge about $12 for each person to enter the park. Access to the path and an educational guide pamphlet are included with this ticket. The cost of guided excursions, which provide extensive information about the geology and history of the volcano, often ranges from $25 to $40 per person. Some tour packages are a practical choice for people who don't want to drive because they also include transportation from Pompeii or Naples.

Different viewpoints of Mount Vesuvius and the surrounding area can be found on several trails that surround the volcano. For example, the "Valle dell'Inferno" track offers a more peaceful and shaded stroll as it winds through the mountain's wooded lower slopes. Despite being longer, this trail is usually regarded as easier because of its steady climb. It's ideal for people who want to explore the area's natural appeal on a less congested path.

It's crucial to review park restrictions and weather predictions when organizing your trip. For safety reasons, the park may close trails during periods of severe wind or precipitation. Because the paths are more peaceful and the light over the Bay of Naples provides a peaceful and unforgettable environment, early morning is frequently the ideal time to visit.

## GUIDED TOURS

To begin your journey, there are various guided tours available that will take you to the active volcano's crater. If you prefer a small group experience or a personalized tour, there are options to suit every taste. Expert guides frequently accompany these tours, giving unique insights into the volcano's geological features, eruption patterns, and the stories of previous inhabitants who lived in its shadow.

The journey to the summit is both informative and thrilling. The routes are well-marked and easily navigable, with frequent pauses along the way where guides explain the different varieties of volcanic rock and the significance of unique formations. As you ascend, you'll have the opportunity to view the changing landscape and the unusual plant species that survive in this volcanic environment. Once at the summit, the panoramic views of the Bay of Naples, the Amalfi Coast, and the surrounding countryside make the effort worthwhile.

Guided tours are frequently an edifying experience, as trained professionals explain the explosion that wrecked Pompeii and other nearby cities. They explain how the volcanic material preserved the towns, providing insight into Roman life. Many trips include transportation to and from Pompeii, making it an ideal choice for those seeking a thorough and seamless experience.

Vesuvius National Park provides well-maintained paths that are open to the public. Visitors can find maps and information points at the park's entry to help them navigate the routes. It is critical to wear adequate footwear and bring enough water because the walk can be strenuous, especially on hot days. Visitors are invited to take their time, enjoying the vistas and learning from the informative markers positioned along the path.

Some trips combine a visit to Mount Vesuvius with a Pompeii excursion, allowing visitors to see both sites in a day. These full-day tours normally begin with a thorough investigation of the ancient city, accompanied by guides who provide context for daily life in Pompeii before the eruption. The competitors are then brought to the base of Vesuvius, where the ascent begins. Combining these experiences helps visitors gain a better understanding of how the volcano's eruption shaped the region and its people.

Private tours are available for individuals who want a more personalized experience. These can be tailored to individual interests, such as focusing on the flora and fauna specific to the volcanic slopes or delving deeper into Vesuvius' historical significance. Personalized tours provide flexibility in schedule, route selection, and additional stops that are less frequented by bigger groups, allowing for a more intimate experience of the area.

Regardless of which option you choose, visiting Mount Vesuvius is an unforgettable and enlightening experience. It provides insight into nature's power and role in molding civilizations, making it a must-see on any Pompeii itinerary. Check the weather forecast before heading to the summit, since circumstances can change fast. To guarantee a seamless and pleasurable visit, double-check the park's hours of operation and availability of guided tours.

## SAFETY GUIDELINES

1. Always examine the weather and volcanic activity bulletins before organizing your trip. Mount Vesuvius is regularly monitored by authorities, and expeditions may be halted if volcanic activity or weather conditions worsen. Staying informed allows you to make the best decisions for your safety.

2. Book Through Certified Tours: Hiring a certified guide assures that you are accompanied by specialists who are familiar with the trails and safety regulations. They are qualified to handle groups and respond to situations, ensuring that you have a safe and informed experience.

3. Wear Appropriate Gear: Proper footwear is essential. The trails can be steep and slick, so excellent traction shoes are needed. Wear comfortable clothes that allow you to move easily, as well as sun and wind protection, to keep you comfortable on the hike.

4. Respect the Environment: It is vital to preserve the natural ecology surrounding Mount Vesuvius. Follow the specified trails and avoid upsetting the plants and

creatures. Avoid collecting rocks or other natural relics, as they are part of the area's geological past.

5. Stay Hydrated and Prepared: The ascent can be physically hard, so bring lots of water and light snacks. Packing a jacket or windbreaker will keep you prepared if the weather changes unexpectedly. Remember that increased altitude might result in colder temperatures, even if it is warm near the base.

6. Follow all signs and instructions: Pay great attention to the safety notices and directions provided by guides. These regulations are intended to keep visitors safe and allow everyone to enjoy the event without incident. Staying behind barricades and away from the crater's edge is critical because the ground can be unstable.

7. Transit plan: There are public transit alternatives available, including buses from Pompeii to the trailhead. They may not run as regularly, so check schedules and plan your return trip accordingly. Renting a car is an alternative for those who prefer a more flexible schedule,

but keep in mind that parking near the trailhead is restricted.

## NEIGHBORING HISTORICAL SITES

## HERCULANEUM

An incredible window into Roman life is provided by Herculaneum, an ancient town that, like its neighbor Pompeii, has been buried under volcanic ash. Compared to Pompeii, the Herculaneum is smaller and more personal, offering visitors the opportunity to examine beautifully preserved structures, stroll through well-maintained streets, and learn about the everyday life of its residents.

Upon visiting Herculaneum, one can see houses with second stories still intact, elaborate mosaics, and colorful frescoes that have withstood the test of time. In contrast to Pompeii, where the devastation caused by the eruption was more rapid, Herculaneum was covered by a layer of ash and muck that consolidated over time. Many buildings were sealed and safeguarded during this process, keeping furniture, wood, and even food scraps details that offer a genuine glimpse into Roman life.

The ancient bathhouses, which demonstrate Roman society's sophisticated engineering, are especially remarkable. Its tenants' comfort and elegance are evident in the exquisite tiling, well-preserved marble, and remarkable heating systems. When strolling around these regions, one can imagine the social and cultural importance that these gathering places once had.

Herculaneum's Villa of the Papyri, a lavish home that once belonged to a wealthy Roman, is another must-see. It is well-known not just for its magnificence but also for the scrolls that were found inside. The wealth of literature found in these scorched papyri some of which are still being analyzed today offers an intriguing glimpse into the scholarly interests of the Roman nobility.

Because of the eruption, the ancient shoreline has been pushed back from the present coast, allowing visitors to examine it. Skeletons discovered in this section of the site provide a heartbreaking account of people who sought shelter but were finally overtaken by the calamity. A more intimate link to the past is provided by visiting this area, which serves as a reminder of the human element hidden beneath the ruins.

A guided tour is advised to maximize a visit to Herculaneum. The ruins are brought to life by experts who enhance the experience by giving anecdotes and historical context. Those who would rather explore at their leisure can also use the audio instructions. To further enhance the appreciation of the town's original magnificence, there are interactive exhibits that offer digital reconstructions of how it looked before the eruption.

The logistics of travel should be taken into account. A simple day trip from Naples is Herculaneum, which is easily accessible by car or train. Because it is less congested than Pompeii, visitors may take in the history and specifics of the ancient town in a more laid-back setting. Though online choices are also available for those who want to save time, tickets can be bought on-site.

Herculaneum has a lot to offer to those who enjoy photography. Its colorful artwork, well-preserved architecture, and ancient atmosphere make it the perfect place to take striking pictures. To safeguard these historic artifacts, visitors should be aware of the rules and refrain from taking flash photos near delicate mosaics and frescoes.

## STABIAE

In contrast to Pompeii and Herculaneum, Stabiae provides an enthralling look into ancient Roman life. Luxurious villas that originally belonged to wealthy Roman residents can be seen in this lesser-known location along the shore, depicting a leisurely and luxurious lifestyle. The region's intellect and artistic talent prior to Mount Vesuvius' devastating eruption are demonstrated by the archeological treasures found here.

Stabiae is home to a number of opulent homes that are all beautifully decorated with elaborate mosaics and paintings that have been marvelously maintained. Among the most prominent are the Villa San Marco and Villa Arianna, which include expansive courtyards, hot springs, and fine dining rooms that provide light on the period's architectural prowess. As you stroll around these areas, it's simple to picture the opulence and sophistication that defined the lives of their original occupants.

The site's historical appeal is enhanced by its lofty location, which provides expansive views of the Bay of Naples. In contrast to other archeological sites, Stabiae's peaceful setting enables visitors to take their time exploring, taking in the details, and admiring the workmanship without being surrounded by people. In addition to providing a glimpse into the past, the ruins serve as a reminder of the area's timeless natural beauty.

Stabiae is a hidden gem for tourists and history buffs alike. The villas offer a close-up view of Roman leisure culture, showing how the wealthy lived, partied, and decorated their homes to be both opulent and comfortable. Every feature of magnificent villas, from the elaborately painted walls to the roomy gardens, reflects the heyday of Roman art and architecture.

**ANTHONY BOLDS**

## OPLONTIS

Situated close to Pompeii in the shadow of Mount Vesuvius, Oplontis provides an intriguing window into the lavish way of life in ancient Rome. Known mostly for the Villa of Poppaea, this archeological site features a magnificent home thought to have belonged to Emperor Nero's wife, Poppaea Sabina. Oplontis shows the serene, private side of Roman life, which is marked by luxury and elegance, in contrast to Pompeii's busy streets and public areas.

A masterwork of Roman architecture, the Villa of Poppaea emphasizes beauty and majesty. Its elaborate paintings, which include vibrant colors and legendary motifs that showcase the artistic talents of the era, are visible as you explore its vast layout. With their elaborate geometric patterns, tranquil landscapes, and lush gardens, these frescoes offer a glimpse into the daily lives and aesthetic preferences of Rome's aristocracy.

As guests move through the villa's rooms, they will come across a gorgeously planned peristyle garden with decorative plants and columns all around it. This open courtyard provided a calm setting away from the bustle of the city, making it a haven for rest. A monument to the Romans' love of leisure and socializing, the villa also had several warm baths outside the garden. For the wealthy, these baths which featured both hot and cold rooms were necessary because they symbolized luxury and prestige.

Oplontis recounts the story of daily living in addition to architecture and art. The villa's use in trade and the prosperous economy of the area before Mount Vesuvius' eruption in 79 AD is demonstrated by the remnants of storage rooms containing amphorae, which are ancient vessels used to transport wine and oil. Together with the tools and household objects that have been preserved, these artifacts paint a clear picture of Roman home life and their networks of commerce.

In contrast to the busy ruins of Pompeii, a visit to Oplontis offers the chance to see a more subdued aspect of Roman history. Oplontis is a serene haven that embodies the elegance and calm desired by the Roman aristocracy, whereas Pompeii was a bustling metropolis. Visitors are encouraged to ponder the beauty of a bygone era in this area where art, architecture, and nature all coexist harmoniously.

Guided tours provide visitors to Oplontis a better understanding of the architectural and historical significance of the villa. The everyday activities of its residents, the meaning of the paintings, and the effects of the eruption that permanently altered this environment are all explained by informed guides. Visitors may see the home as it was in the past thanks to interactive exhibits and virtual reconstructions made possible by modern technology, which enhances the experience even more.

Oplontis is easily accessible, with amenities that meet a range of needs and obvious signage. Because of its good upkeep, visitors can easily explore the site's highlights and enjoy its preserved beauty.

## DAY TRIPS

## NAPLES AND ITS TREASURES

Pompeii is more than just ancient remains; it's also a starting point for exploring Naples, a city full of historical, artistic, and culinary treasures. A quick day journey to Naples reveals a bustling city where the past and current live side by side in harmony. The trip starts with a quick ride from Pompeii, which takes you directly to the center of this famous city.

Naples is home to treasures such as the National Archaeological Museum, which displays relics from Pompeii, such as elaborate statues and mosaics that offer a more profound insight into Roman life. There is a clear link between the two ancient locations as you explore the museum and see artifacts that were originally used to decorate the Pompeiian villas.

The actual city is a vibrant center of customs and culture. As you stroll down its historic streets, you'll come across artisanal stores, busy markets, and cathedrals that date back centuries. The well-known Spaccanapoli, a lengthy, winding street that runs through the center of Naples, is the ideal place to experience the regional cuisine. With a genuine flavor of tradition in every bite, Neapolitan pizza is more than simply a meal here it's an experience.

The Capodimonte Museum and Royal Palace provide art lovers with a window into the lavish history of Naples' nobility. For anybody interested in Italy's cultural legacy, these locations are must-visits because they contain collections from some of the most well-known artists in the nation.

Walking along the coastline offers breathtaking views of Mount Vesuvius towering over the Bay of Naples. Natural beauty and ancient forces have molded the region over millennia, and its famous landscape serves as a reminder of its tremendous past.

A visit to the famous Castel dell'Ovo, a seaside fortification that has been an important part of the city's defenses for centuries, is another opportunity Naples provides. Its moniker, "Egg Castle," is derived from the myth that the Roman poet Virgil concealed an egg within its foundations and foretold that the city would endure as long as the egg was intact. While exploring its halls offers sweeping vistas of the coastline, it also offers insight into Naples' past.

Naples has another delectable Italian cuisine for those seeking a flavor of the past. Sfogliatella, a sweet pastry with a crunchy, flaky texture, is served in local cafés, and gelato kiosks to entice you to enjoy Italy's well-known frozen delight. Markets and street vendors are ablaze with the aroma of seafood, fresh produce, and other local specialties, beckoning tourists to experience the flavors of the city.

## THE AMALFI COAST

Start your tour in Sorrento, a town noted for its vivid citrus trees and cliffside views. Walking through Sorrento's tiny streets, you'll come across artisanal stores, cafés, and a vibrant environment that combines local culture with the attractiveness of a seaside town. Sorrento is also a starting point for boat cruises, which provide panoramic views of the coast and surrounding islands.

ANTHONY BOLDS

A bit further along the coast, the town of Positano emerges with its colorful buildings sliding down the mountainside. This iconic location is great for a relaxing day spent strolling along the beach, exploring tiny stores, and eating delicious seafood at a coastal restaurant. Positano's appeal stems from its blend of natural beauty and stylish ambiance, making it a must-see destination for any traveler.

Amalfi is another treasure on this coastal path, with a rich historical past. The town's cathedral, with its spectacular medieval architecture, stands as a reminder of its rich history. Wander through the town's alleys to locate local cuisines and crafts reflecting regional customs. Amalfi is also a popular destination for boat trips, which allow visitors to explore the coast's magnificent cliffs and hidden bays from a different angle.

Ravello, located further down the coast, is a hilltop village known for its beautiful gardens and scenic terraces. Ravello provides a peaceful refuge, ideal for unwinding with a view of the coast and sea. Ravello's medieval homes, such as Villa Rufolo and Villa Cimbrone, are noted for their scenic settings and peaceful ambiance, making it an ideal destination for individuals interested in history, art, and nature.

## SORRENTO AND CAPRI

Day tours from Pompeii to Sorrento and Capri combine pleasant activities with stunning seaside scenery. You may travel from Pompeii to Sorrento, a town renowned for its lively atmosphere and breathtaking seaside vistas, by rail or automobile. Here, tourists may meander through tiny alleyways dotted with stores offering regional handicrafts and delectable Italian fare, such as freshly squeezed lemons and homemade gelato.

Eating at one of the many restaurants by the water in Marina Grande, Sorrento's harbor, is the ideal way to watch fishing boats arrive. It's a pleasure to explore the town's historic core, which is full of charming lanes and architectural treasures. It's a chance to engage with the local heritage by touring sites like the old cloisters or the Cathedral of Sorrento. Spending time here is a must-do for any day trip since it combines culture, cuisine, and coastal charm.

Ferries travel to Capri, an island known for its exquisite mood and stunning scenery, from Sorrento. The view of Capri's cliffs rising from the azure ocean is incredibly mesmerizing as the ferry draws closer. When they first arrive, tourists frequently go to Capri's main square, the Piazzetta, which is a bustling center with many cafés. It's a wonderful place to unwind and take in the atmosphere of the island.

Views of secluded grottos and imposing rock formations like the Faraglioni can be seen on a boat cruise around the island for a more daring experience. One of the highlights of these excursions is the Blue Grotto, a well-known sea cave that is distinguished by its luminous blue waters that give the impression of being on another planet. To further explore the island, take a chairlift trip up Monte Solaro to Anacapri, a little community on a higher area of the island that offers a different side of Capri with calmer streets and expansive vistas.

# CHAPTER 8

## CULTURAL IMMERSION

## FESTIVALS AND EVENTS CALENDAR

### Pompeii's Summer Festival

Every summer, Pompeii becomes a hotbed of artistic expression, with performances that breathe new life into the old ruins. The Summer Festival is a series of concerts, plays, and cultural exhibitions hosted at the ancient amphitheater. These activities draw both locals and visitors, allowing them to experience music and drama in a centuries-old setting. The atmosphere is both electrifying and nostalgic, creating an unforgettable evening beneath the stars.

### Ludi Pompeiani: Games and Performances.

Ludi Pompeiani provides a unique opportunity to learn about ancient Roman culture. This event reenacts traditional Roman games, including theatrical performances and gladiatorial shows, in the same amphitheater where they were held over two thousand years ago. Visitors learn about Roman entertainment and how these events influenced public life. The performances are intended to be both instructive and engaging, giving audiences a better understanding of the city's rich history.

## Religious Ceremonies and Processions

Throughout the year, Pompeii organizes several religious festivities based on ancient rituals performed in the city's temples. These celebrations frequently feature processions in which participants dress in ancient costumes, resurrecting the spiritual rituals of the early residents. One notable ceremony is the Feast of Venus, which honors Pompeii's patron goddess. It combines modern festivities with ancient components, providing insight into how the Romans honored their deities.

## Annual Wine Festival

Pompeii's rich volcanic soil produces some of the best grapes, and the Annual Wine Festival commemorates this legacy. The event invites wine fans to taste diverse local wines, savor culinary pleasures, and learn about winemaking techniques passed down through generations. The event brings together wineries, chefs, and artisans, making it an ideal destination for people looking for real local experiences.

## Antique Fair and Artisan Market

Pompeii features antique fairs and artisan markets throughout the year, attracting collectors and art lovers from all around the region. These markets provide homemade items, antiques, and artwork that reflect the city's classical past. Shoppers can explore stalls set up against the backdrop of ancient ruins, which combine modern business with historical beauty. It's an opportunity to support local artisans while discovering unique things that capture the essence of Pompeii.

## Natale di Pompei - Pompeii's Birthday Celebration

Pompeii's founding anniversary, the Natale di Pompei, is celebrated every October. This event features historical excursions, art exhibitions, and activities commemorating the city's lengthy history. It's an opportunity to reflect on

**ANTHONY BOLDS**

Pompeii's evolution over time, from its days as a vibrant Roman city to its rebirth as a world-renowned archeological site. Participants enjoy guided tours, special speeches, and exhibitions featuring current findings, making the event both educational and exciting.

## Winter events and Christmas festivities.

During the holiday season, Pompeii transforms into a festive destination, complete with light displays, traditional markets, and festive festivities. The city has a warm and welcoming atmosphere, which is ideal for celebrating the holidays. The winter season offers a more tranquil experience, allowing tourists to explore the ancient site and surrounding streets at their leisure. Seasonal concerts and art pieces enhance the festive atmosphere, creating a magnificent backdrop for tourists.

## MUSIC, THEATER, AND ARTS SCENE

Pompeii's amphitheater, one of the oldest of its kind, represents the city's rich theatrical legacy. This vast building, capable of hosting thousands, was once filled with the sounds of ancient Roman spectacles such as gladiatorial battles and dramatic performances. Today, visitors roaming amid its stone tiers might imagine the grandeur and excitement that once filled this area. The architecture tells a tale, demonstrating how the Romans planned their entertainment spaces to maximize audience engagement.

Music played an important role in Pompeii's cultural fabric. Frescoes discovered in the remains portray musicians playing instruments like as the lyre, flute, and tambourine, emphasizing the importance of music in both everyday life and special occasions. According to evidence, both public and private festivities would have been accompanied by spirited musical performances, adding to the ambiance of the city's social and spiritual events. This musical legacy is carried on now through modern concerts and events organized at the archaeological site, where musicians attempt to reproduce the sounds and rhythms of ancient Pompeii.

The artistic side of Pompeii extends beyond theater and music to visual arts, which are exceptionally well-preserved among the ruins. The city's mansions and public buildings have bright paintings and mosaics depicting scenes from mythology, nature, and everyday life. Walking through these spaces provides insight into the artistic abilities and aesthetic tastes of the time. Each item, with its complex detailing and vibrant hues, exemplifies the skill of ancient painters who strived to create beauty and communicate stories through their work.

Pompeii's art culture continues to inspire contemporary artists. Today, exhibitions and workshops are held around the site, encouraging people to experiment with traditional techniques and discover their creative expressions. The city's continuous role as an arts and culture hub attracts artists and performers from all over the world, each contributing their interpretation of Pompeii's historical legacy to the present artistic dialogue.

## LOCAL CUSTOMS AND ETIQUETTE

First and foremost, it is crucial to respect the archaeological sites. It is forbidden to touch or climb on the meticulously preserved ancient ruins and antiquities. In addition to following any signs or staff directions, visitors should stay on the specified walkways. Every component of the site is a piece of a bigger historical puzzle, so it's crucial to avoid taking anything away, not even tiny stones.

In general, photography is permitted, but consideration is required. Certain locations may not allow flash photography, particularly those with fragile structures and old frescoes. By abiding by these guidelines, the integrity of the building and art is preserved. Be careful not to block walkways or disrupt other guests' experiences when shooting pictures.

To show respect for the historical place and the local culture, dress comfortably and modestly. It is appropriate to wear light clothes that cover the knees and shoulders, especially if you intend to visit places of worship or places where modesty is valued. Because of the rough terrain and cobblestone streets, comfortable shoes are also a must.

In Italy, greetings are culturally significant. When engaging with locals, a kind grin and a simple "Buongiorno" (Good morning) or "Buonasera" (Good evening) are welcomed. It's customary to say "Grazie" (thank you) to employees when you first enter a business or restaurant.

Italian customs govern eating patterns in Pompeii and the surrounding areas, where meals are valued at social gatherings. It's normal to wait for everyone's food to arrive before beginning when dining at a restaurant. Additionally, as chefs take delight in their culinary creations, don't request food adjustments unless required. Tipping is appreciated when service is outstanding, but it is not required. It's usually enough to round up the amount or spend a few euros.

The best way to enjoy Pompeii's rich artistic and historical heritage is to be mindful. Being conscious of noise levels is part of this. The historic remains serve as a site for introspection, education, and discovery. Respecting other users and the website itself is demonstrated by keeping voices at a moderate volume.

When buying mementos, think about helping out small companies and local artists. In addition to being distinctive mementos, locally made or handcrafted goods support the local economy.

Knowing Pompeii's historical history gives any visit more significance. Roman society, customs, and daily life can be better understood by reading about its history or going on a guided tour. Stories that have been passed down through the years are frequently shared by the locals and tour guides, adding a personal touch to the trip.

## LEARNING BASIC ITALIAN PHRASES

Start with greetings and pleasantries. A simple Buongiorno (Good morning) or Buonasera (Good evening) can be a great way to start any conversation. When saying goodbye, Arrivederci (Goodbye) or Ciao (Hi/Bye) works well, depending on the level of formality. Remembering to say Per favore (Please) and Grazie (Thank you) is also essential when asking for something or expressing gratitude. These small words can go a long way in creating a friendly and respectful interaction.

When ordering food or drinks, phrases like Vorrei un caffè, per favore (I would like a coffee, please) or Posso avere il conto? (May I have the bill?) come in handy. The local cuisine is a major part of the Pompeii experience, and being able to order in Italian makes the meal more special. Knowing how to ask for water (Acqua) or wine (Vino) is also helpful, especially when enjoying the local specialties.

Navigating through the archaeological park or city streets, you might need to ask for directions. Using phrases like

ANTHONY BOLDS

Dov'è…? (Where is…?) or Quanto costa…? (How much does it cost?) can assist in finding your way or understanding prices. Whether looking for the entrance to a specific site or locating a restaurant, these questions are practical and useful.

Politeness is key in Italian culture. Saying Mi scusi (Excuse me) when trying to get someone's attention or asking for help shows courtesy. If you need assistance or information, starting your request with this phrase makes interactions smoother. Another important phrase is Parla inglese? (Do you speak English?), which can be very useful when you need help but aren't confident in your Italian. Many people will appreciate your attempt to speak Italian and may respond with enthusiasm.

If you plan on visiting shops or markets, understanding numbers and prices will be beneficial. Learning numbers up to ten (Uno, due, tre…) and phrases like Quanti anni ha questo oggetto? (How old is this item?) can make shopping and bartering an interesting cultural exchange.

Locals often appreciate when tourists try to communicate in their language, even if it's just for basic transactions.

## PARTICIPATING IN COMMUNITY ACTIVITIES

Participating in community events during your vacation to Pompeii provides an exceptional opportunity to connect with the local culture and people. The city and surrounding region organize a number of events and customs that visitors can attend to obtain a better knowledge of life in this historic location.

Visitors could come across local markets where inhabitants offer fresh vegetables, handcrafted crafts, and traditional cuisine. These markets provide a real view into people's daily lives and an opportunity to sample local delicacies. Engaging with vendors and fellow shoppers allows visitors to feel the warmth and friendliness of the town.

Seasonal festivities are another attraction. These festivities frequently include parades, musical performances, and traditional dances that highlight the region's heritage. Visitors can participate in these festivals and learn about old and modern traditions. Such celebrations provide visitors with a firsthand look at how Pompeii honors its history while celebrating current life.

Seminars and classes are available, allowing tourists to engage in pottery making, fresco painting, or cooking sessions to learn about Roman food. These hands-on experiences provide a creative and educational approach to discovering Pompeii's rich legacy, led by trained artists who share their knowledge.

Community-led guided tours offer an opportunity to see Pompeii's historical sites from a local perspective. These excursions, sometimes organized by local clubs or cultural organizations, not only show visitors the city's iconic ruins but also introduce them to lesser-known locations, stories, and traditions passed down through centuries. Joining such trips develops a sense of community and connection with both the guides and the other travelers.

Volunteer opportunities are offered to people who want to give back. Participating in local conservation efforts or community clean-up days can be a satisfying approach to help preserve Pompeii's treasures. By participating, tourists become temporary members of the community, helping to preserve the area's historical and natural beauty.

Music and theatrical performances, which are frequently staged in old amphitheaters or open-air locations, are another way to connect with the local culture. These events allow local artists to share their talents and stories, enabling tourists to become a part of Pompeii's thriving artistic community. Attending these shows not only benefits the local community but also provides a rich cultural experience.

# CHAPTER 9

## CULINARY JOURNEY

## TOP RESTAURANTS AND CAFÉS

1. Ristorante President

Location: Via Sacra, Pompeii

Average Price: $30 - $60 per person

Ristorante President stands out for its refined take on traditional Neapolitan dishes. With an emphasis on fresh, local ingredients, this elegant venue offers a variety of options, including seafood risotto and homemade pasta dishes. The chef's attention to detail brings a burst of flavor to every bite, making it a memorable dining experience. It is advised to make reservations, particularly during the busiest travel seasons.

Tip: Try the tasting menu for a diverse experience of the region's best flavors. It's an ideal way to savor multiple dishes in one visit.

2. Add'u Mimi

Location: Via Roma, Pompeii

Average Price: $15 - $40 per person

A family-owned gem, Add'u Mimi offers a cozy atmosphere perfect for enjoying hearty Italian classics like Margherita pizza, spaghetti carbonara, and fresh salads. The outdoor seating area provides a relaxed environment, making it a great spot to unwind after exploring the ruins. The menu is affordable, offering both quick bites and full meals, ensuring that every traveler finds something they'll enjoy.

Tip: Visit during lunchtime to take advantage of the fixed-price menu, which offers a selection of dishes at a reasonable rate.

3. Trammiere Pompeiano

Location: Via Villa dei Misteri, Pompeii

Average Price: $10 - $30 per person

This café offers a casual yet authentic taste of local culture with its simple yet delicious offerings. Trammiere Pompeiano is a convenient stop close to the archaeological site, making it a perfect break during your visit. With options ranging from freshly made paninis to refreshing gelato, it caters to various tastes without breaking the bank.

Tip: Pair your meal with a classic espresso or cappuccino for a true Italian café experience. The gelato flavors change daily, so it's worth stopping by more than once.

4. Il Machiavelli

Location: Piazza Anfiteatro, Pompeii

Average Price: $25 - $50 per person

Set in a charming piazza, Il Machiavelli brings a sophisticated touch to dining in Pompeii. The restaurant specializes in dishes like slow-cooked lamb, seafood platters, and an impressive selection of wines from local vineyards. With its ambient lighting and welcoming service, it's a great choice for both lunch and dinner.

ANTHONY BOLDS

Tip: Request a table on the terrace for a view of the bustling square while you enjoy your meal. It's the perfect spot for people-watching as you sip on a glass of fine Italian wine.

5. Viva lo Re

Location: Via Plinio, Pompeii

Average Price: $20 - $45 per person

Viva lo Re offers an innovative menu combining local ingredients with contemporary culinary techniques. The menu varies seasonally, ensuring fresh flavors year-round. With options like wood-fired pizzas and grilled vegetables, it's an ideal spot for vegetarians and vegans looking to explore Italian cuisine.

Tip: The house-made desserts, particularly the tiramisu, are a must-try. It's a lovely way to finish off your dinner with something sweet.

6. Pasticceria De Vivo dal 1955

Location: Via Roma, Pompeii

Average Price: $5 - $15 per person

Pasticceria De Vivo is a beloved local pastry shop that has been serving traditional Italian desserts since 1955. With a variety of pastries, cakes, and gelato, it's a must-visit for anyone with a sweet tooth. The inviting atmosphere and friendly service make it a pleasant place to relax and enjoy a snack.

Tip: Sample the sfogliatella, a flaky pastry filled with sweet ricotta a classic Neapolitan delight that pairs well with a cappuccino.

7. La Bettola del Gusto

Location: Via Sacra, Pompeii

Average Price: $30 - $55 per person

This well-known restaurant is famous for its fusion of modern and traditional dishes. With a focus on presentation and flavor, La Bettola del Gusto serves options like truffle pasta and grilled fish, paired perfectly with local wines. The contemporary setting provides a comfortable and stylish atmosphere, making it suitable for a relaxed evening meal.

Tip: Book ahead to secure a spot, as it's a popular choice among both locals and tourists.

## STREET FOOD DELIGHTS

Begin your trip at Pompeii Archaeological Park, where you may find traditional food vendors at the entrance. Pizza a Portafoglio (folded pizza) is a popular snack here, as it is both portable and flavorful, making it ideal for on-the-go consumption. These hand-sized pizzas are normally priced between €3 and €5, making them a cost-effective option. Look for stands where locals congregate, as this is frequently indicative of quality and freshness.

Another must-try is Sfogliatella, a crispy pastry stuffed with sweet ricotta. This delicacy, popular in Campania, may be purchased at several bakeries along Via Roma. Expect to pay between €2 and €4 for each pastry. To get the best version, come early in the day when they are freshly baked, ensuring a warm and flaky pleasure.

For a savory option, try Arancini fried rice balls packed with ragù, cheese, or peas. These are sold in most snack stores surrounding Piazza Anfiteatro and typically cost between €2.50-€4 each. For the finest experience, choose freshly fried, as they provide the ideal crisp and flavor combo.

While walking through the streets near the Forum, keep a lookout for vendors selling Zeppole. These delicate, fried dough balls coated with sugar are popular with visitors. A dish normally costs between €3 and €5, and it is an excellent sweet treat for touring. It's best to eat them hot, fresh from the fryer, to appreciate their light, fluffy texture.

Frittura di Paranza, a blend of little fried fish served in paper cones, is a must-try for seafood aficionados. You can buy this specialty near the Porta Marina entrance, with costs ranging from €6 to €8. This choice is ideal for people who wish to experience the region's maritime delicacies while strolling along Pompeii's historical trails. A nice idea is to request lemon slices, as citrus enhances the freshness of fish.

Visit the gelato kiosks strewn throughout Pompeii. Traditional flavors such as pistachio, hazelnut, and lemon are popular, with prices ranging between €2 and €4 per scoop. For the greatest experience, look for stores that say "artigianale" (artisan) on their signs, which frequently suggest handcrafted gelato made with high-quality ingredients.

To round out your street food trip, visit a Panino Napoletano vendor, where these stuffed bread rolls provide a hearty option. They are typically loaded with salami, cheese, and, sometimes, olives, and are ideal for a quick lunch. These can be found near the train station or on Via Plinio for about €5 to €7. They're filling enough to keep you going after a long day of exploring.

# WINE REGIONS AND VINEYARD TOURS

## Wine Regions Around Pompeii

The fertile land surrounding Mount Vesuvius has supported vineyards for centuries, creating wines that are distinctively robust and aromatic. This region, known as the Vesuvian Wine Zone, produces the famous Lacryma Christi ("Tears of Christ") wine, a favorite among locals and visitors alike. The wine's legend adds an intriguing layer to its complex flavor profile, which features hints of mineral notes from the volcanic soil. Visitors can explore this history while savoring its unique tastes.

## Popular Vineyards to Visit

1. Cantina del Vesuvio Winery

Location: Situated on the slopes of Mount Vesuvius, this vineyard offers panoramic views of both the volcano and the Bay of Naples. It's easily accessible from Pompeii, making it a convenient option.

Tours and Tastings: They offer guided tours where visitors can stroll through the vineyards and learn about the cultivation methods passed down through generations. The experience includes tastings of their best wines paired with local appetizers, enhancing the flavors.

Pricing: A guided tour with tasting starts at around $45 per person. Options for a more in-depth experience, including a full meal with wine pairing, are available for approximately $70.

Tips: Booking in advance is recommended, especially during the peak season. Be sure to wear comfortable shoes as the vineyard terrain can be uneven.

2. Mastroberardino Winery

Location: Just a short drive from Pompeii, this renowned winery is located in the town of Atripalda. Known for reviving ancient grape varieties, Mastroberardino is a must-visit for wine enthusiasts interested in historical winemaking techniques.

Tours and Tastings: The vineyard offers a comprehensive tour that delves into the history of the winery, including a look at its historic cellars. Visitors can enjoy tastings of various wines, including their iconic Taurasi, paired with regional cheese and cured meats.

Pricing: Standard tours start at $55 per person, with an option for a premium tasting experience costing around $90.

Tips: Consider scheduling your visit during the harvest season (September-October) for a chance to see the winemaking process in action.

3. Sorrentino Vini

Location: Nestled along the scenic roads leading to Vesuvius National Park, this family-owned vineyard offers an intimate and authentic Italian experience.

Tours and Tastings: Sorrentino Vini specializes in organic wines, and their tour includes an educational walk through their vineyards, focusing on organic farming practices. The tour concludes with a wine-tasting session featuring their organic Lacryma Christi wine, accompanied by a selection of local produce.

Pricing: Prices start at $40 for a basic tasting tour, while a more immersive option with a traditional meal is available for $75.

Tips: The vineyard is a fantastic choice for those looking to understand sustainable wine production. Visitors can also explore nearby hiking trails in the national park before or after their visit.

## COOKING CLASSES AND FOOD WORKSHOPS

### Cooking Classes in Pompeii

1. Traditional Neapolitan Pizza Making

Location: Pizzeria Delizia, Pompeii Historic Center

Price: $50 per person

Learn the secrets of crafting the perfect Neapolitan pizza in a hands-on workshop led by experienced local chefs. This class covers everything from kneading dough to achieving the ideal crispiness in a wood-fired oven. Participants will also enjoy their own freshly made pizza, topped with regional ingredients like mozzarella di bufala and San Marzano tomatoes.

Tip: Book in advance to secure a spot, especially during peak tourist seasons. Comfortable clothing is recommended as you'll be working with flour and dough.

2. Pasta from Scratch: The Art of Homemade Pasta

Location: Villa dei Sapori, just outside Pompeii's main entrance

Price: $65 per person (includes wine tasting)

Delve into the art of making pasta by hand, guided by an expert chef. Participants will craft different types of pasta, such as fettuccine and ravioli, and explore various fillings and sauces typical of the Campania region. The class concludes with a meal where guests enjoy their creations paired with local wines.

Tip: Opt for the morning session to make the most of a full day in Pompeii. This class is perfect for those looking to expand their skills in Italian cooking.

3. Ancient Roman Cooking Experience

Location: Pompeii Archaeological Park

**ANTHONY BOLDS**

Price: $80 per person

This unique workshop transports participants back in time, exploring recipes and techniques used during the height of the Roman Empire. Led by culinary historians, the class provides a fascinating look at how ancient Romans prepared meals using ingredients like garum, honey, and fresh herbs. Guests will recreate dishes based on historical texts and enjoy a feast reminiscent of ancient banquets.

Tip: This experience is ideal for history enthusiasts and those curious about ancient culinary practices. Comfortable shoes are advised, as participants may explore parts of the archaeological site during the workshop.

### Food Workshops and Tastings

1. Wine and Olive Oil Tasting Workshop

Location: Tenuta Vesuvio, a short drive from Pompeii

Price: $45 per person (includes transportation from Pompeii)

Participants in this workshop will discover the wine and olive oil production process, sampling local varieties such as Lacryma Christi wine and cold-pressed olive oils. The session includes a guided tasting and a tour of the vineyard and olive grove, offering a chance to understand the landscape's role in shaping these products.

Tip: Ideal for those with limited time, as the workshop lasts two hours. Combine it with a morning visit to Pompeii's ruins for a full-day experience.

2. Gelato Making Class

Location: Gelateria del Corso, Pompeii Town Center

Price: $40 per person

A delightful option for families or anyone with a sweet tooth, this gelato-making class covers the basics of creating authentic Italian gelato. Participants will experiment with classic and seasonal flavors, learning techniques to achieve the perfect texture. The workshop ends with a tasting session where you can sample your gelato creations.

Tip: This class is suitable for all ages. Children often receive a discount, making it a fun and educational activity for families.

3. The Art of Mozzarella: Cheese-Making Workshop

Location: Fattoria Della Campagna, a local farm near Pompeii

Price: $55 per person

Experience the art of mozzarella-making firsthand in this interactive workshop hosted at a working farm. Participants will learn about the process of curdling milk, shaping mozzarella balls, and the significance of this iconic cheese in Italian cuisine. Guests can also enjoy a farm-to-table lunch featuring fresh mozzarella and other local products.

Tip: Perfect for cheese lovers, this workshop offers a chance to understand the farm's role in producing high-quality dairy products. Consider bringing a cooler bag if you plan to take fresh mozzarella home.

## Booking Information and Tips

1. It's advisable to book classes and workshops online before your trip to guarantee availability, as many of these experiences are popular, particularly in the summer months.

For most workshops, transportation options are available upon request, making it easier to reach locations outside the archaeological park.

2. Classes typically provide all necessary materials and aprons, so visitors only need to arrive with a passion for cooking and an appetite for learning.

3. Look for discounts or package deals that combine cooking classes with other activities like vineyard tours or guided walks through Pompeii's ruins. These bundles often provide a richer, more economical experience.

# CHAPTER 10

## WHERE TO STAY

## LUXURY HOTELS AND RESORTS

1. Hotel Forum

Location: Via Roma 99, Pompeii

Price Range: $180 - $350 per night

Hours: Check-in: 3 PM, Check-out: 11 AM

Hotel Forum is an exquisite blend of classic design and modern amenities. Located in the heart of Pompeii, this hotel offers easy access to the archaeological sites. Guests can enjoy the serenity of the hotel's private garden, a perfect retreat after a day of exploring. The hotel provides spacious rooms, each equipped with premium bedding, a minibar, and Wi-Fi. Booking a room here includes a complimentary breakfast featuring fresh, local ingredients. For a more personalized experience, consider booking a suite with a terrace that overlooks the lush gardens.

Tip: Make reservations in advance, especially during peak tourist season, to secure the best rates and rooms.

2. Bosco de' Medici Resort

Location: Via Antonio Segni 43, Pompeii

Price Range: $200 - $400 per night

Hours: Check-in: 2 PM, Check-out: 11 AM

Located within a vineyard, Bosco de' Medici Resort provides a tranquil escape with a blend of rustic charm and contemporary comfort. This resort features an outdoor pool, a wellness center, and a restaurant serving farm-to-table dishes that highlight regional flavors. The rooms are spacious, with views of Mount Vesuvius or the resort's vineyard. Guests can also enjoy wine-tasting sessions and vineyard tours, making it an ideal spot for those interested in experiencing the local culture in an intimate setting.

Tip: Take advantage of the resort's cooking classes, where chefs share insights into authentic Italian cuisine.

3. Habita79 Pompeii - MGallery

Location: Via Roma 10, Pompeii

Price Range: $250 - $450 per night

Hours: Check-in: 3 PM, Check-out: 12 PM

This luxury hotel blends contemporary design with elements inspired by Pompeii's ancient history. Habita79 features an elegant rooftop terrace, perfect for dining with panoramic views of the city and Mount Vesuvius. Rooms are elegantly furnished with modern touches, offering a balance of comfort and style. The hotel's wellness center provides a range of services, including massage and sauna options, ideal for relaxation after a day of sightseeing.

Tip: Book a table at the rooftop restaurant during sunset for a stunning view of Mount Vesuvius.

4. Villa Franca Boutique Hotel

Location: Via Villa dei Misteri 11, Pompeii

Price Range: $230 - $400 per night

Hours: Check-in: 2 PM, Check-out: 10 AM

**ANTHONY BOLDS**

Villa Franca Boutique Hotel is a charming spot that provides a warm and personal touch. Each room is individually designed, with a focus on comfort and elegance. The hotel offers a delightful breakfast service with freshly baked goods, ensuring a great start to your day. Located close to the ancient ruins, it offers convenience while maintaining a peaceful atmosphere.

Tip: Ask the front desk about private tours to the archaeological park for a more immersive experience.

5. Pompei Resort

Location: Viale Unità d'Italia 16/A, Pompeii

Price Range: $150 - $350 per night

Hours: Check-in: 2 PM, Check-out: 11 AM

Pompei Resort stands out for its spacious, modern rooms and commitment to guest satisfaction. It features an outdoor garden and a terrace where guests can unwind with a glass of wine. The on-site restaurant serves a menu filled with Italian classics, prepared using locally sourced ingredients. It's a family-friendly choice with options for larger suites to accommodate groups.

Tip: Make use of the complimentary shuttle service to the archaeological sites for added convenience.

6. Hotel Vittoria

Location: Piazza Porta Marina Inferiore 2, Pompeii

Price Range: $160 - $330 per night

Hours: Check-in: 1 PM, Check-out: 11 AM

Hotel Vittoria boasts a prime location right at the entrance of the Pompeii ruins. With its convenient spot, guests can easily access the historical sites and return for a restful night in cozy, well-furnished rooms. The hotel's restaurant offers Italian dishes with a focus on fresh seafood. Guests can also enjoy an aperitivo on the terrace while soaking in the views of the ancient city.

Tip: Opt for the rooms with balconies for a more scenic experience.

7. Grand Hotel La Sonrisa

Location: Via Stabia 500, Sant'Antonio Abate (near Pompeii)

Price Range: $220 - $500 per night

Hours: Check-in: 3 PM, Check-out: 11 AM

A short drive from Pompeii, Grand Hotel La Sonrisa is a majestic property with a regal ambiance. It offers spacious suites adorned with antique furniture, creating a feeling of timeless elegance. The hotel features lush gardens, a large outdoor pool, and a wellness spa. Perfect for weddings or special occasions, this grand hotel provides a luxurious experience with personalized service.

Tip: If you're planning a romantic getaway, book one of their honeymoon suites, which includes special amenities and services.

ANTHONY BOLDS

## MID-RANGE COMFORTS

1. Hotel Diana Pompei

Price Range: $90 - $120 per night

Location: Via Sacra 29, Pompeii, Italy

Opening Hours: Check-in from 2:00 PM, Check-out by 11:00 AM

Description: This charming hotel offers a cozy atmosphere with modern amenities, including complimentary Wi-Fi and an on-site bar. Its proximity to the archaeological site (a 10-minute walk) and the local train station makes it a convenient choice for exploring Pompeii and nearby towns.

Tips: Request a room with a garden view for a tranquil experience. To guarantee the greatest prices, reservations should be made well in advance, particularly during the busiest travel seasons.

2. Villa Franca

Price Range: $80 - $110 per night

Location: Via Diomede 1, Pompeii, Italy

Opening Hours: Reception available 24 hours

Description: Villa Franca provides a warm, welcoming environment with spacious rooms and a delightful garden area where guests can unwind after a day of exploration. The property is family-run, ensuring a personalized touch throughout your stay.

Tips: Ideal for families and couples looking for a homely ambiance close to Pompeii's historic attractions. The complimentary breakfast includes local specialties and fresh produce.

3. Hotel Palma

Price Range: $100 - $140 per night

Location: Via Piave 15, Pompeii, Italy

Opening Hours: Check-in from 3:00 PM, Check-out by 10:30 AM

Description: Situated just steps away from the main entrance to the ruins, Hotel Palma offers elegant, air-conditioned rooms equipped with all the essentials for a comfortable stay. Guests can enjoy a rooftop terrace with views of Mount Vesuvius, perfect for a relaxing evening.

Tips: Opt for the rooms with balcony access for a great view. The hotel staff can also arrange guided tours and transportation for convenience.

4. B&B Pompei Welcome

Price Range: $70 - $95 per night

Location: Viale Giuseppe Mazzini 83, Pompeii, Italy

Opening Hours: Reception is open from 7:00 AM - 10:00 PM

Description: This bed and breakfast combines affordability with comfort, offering cozy rooms and a hearty breakfast each morning. Located close to the city center, it's easy to access local eateries and public transport.

# ANTHONY BOLDS

Tips: Ask the staff for recommendations on local dining spots for an authentic culinary experience. Late check-out is available upon request.

5. Hotel Forum

Price Range: $120 - $160 per night

Location: Via Roma 99, Pompeii, Italy

Opening Hours: Reception available 24 hours

Description: Known for its central location, Hotel Forum stands out with its stylish rooms and lush courtyard garden. The on-site restaurant serves a variety of Italian dishes, and the hotel offers easy access to the ruins and other attractions in the area.

Tips: Consider dining at the hotel's restaurant for a taste of classic Neapolitan cuisine. Reserving a table for dinner in advance is a good idea, especially during weekends.

6. Hotel Maiuri

Price Range: $90 - $130 per night

Location: Via Casone 2, Pompeii, Italy

Opening Hours: Check-in from 2:00 PM, Check-out by 11:00 AM

Description: A family-friendly option, Hotel Maiuri offers comfortable rooms and friendly service. The property includes a garden and an outdoor seating area where guests can relax. It's located slightly away from the busiest areas, providing a quiet retreat while remaining accessible.

Tips: The hotel provides bicycles for rent, which are a fantastic way to explore the nearby streets. Ask for maps and suggestions at the front desk for a customized experience.

7. Hotel Iside

Price Range: $75 - $115 per night

Location: Via Minutella 27, Pompeii, Italy

Opening Hours: Check-in from 3:00 PM, Check-out by 11:00 AM

Description: A perfect choice for travelers wanting comfort at an affordable price, Hotel Iside offers well-kept rooms and a friendly atmosphere. The hotel has a spacious parking area, making it ideal for those traveling by car. It's also just a short walk from the entrance to Pompeii's ruins.

Tips: Early booking ensures availability, as the hotel tends to fill up during summer. The staff is knowledgeable about the local area, providing excellent tips for sightseeing and dining.

## BUDGET-FRIENDLY ACCOMMODATIONS

1. Hotel Diana Pompei

Price Range: Between $60 to $100 per night, around

Location: Via Sacra 29, 80045 Pompei, Italy

Check-in/Check-out Hours: Check-in from 2 PM; check-out until 11 AM

Description: This family-run hotel offers clean rooms and warm hospitality. Situated near the city center, it's just a short walk from the main archaeological sites.

Tips: Book early to secure the best rates, and request a room with a garden view for a quieter experience.

2. B&B Elena

Price Range: Around $50 - $80 per night

Location: Via Minutella 43, 80045 Pompei, Italy

Check-in/Check-out Hours: Check-in from 1 PM; check-out until 10 AM

Description: A cozy bed and breakfast that provides comfortable accommodations and a homemade breakfast. It's close to public transportation, making it easy to explore the area.

Tips: Take advantage of the host's local knowledge for dining and sightseeing recommendations.

3. Pompei Boutique Inn

Price Range: $55 to $90 per night, around

Location: Via Lepanto 137, 80045 Pompei, Italy

Check-in/Check-out Hours: Check-in from 3 PM; check-out until 10 AM

Description: Offering stylish rooms with modern amenities, this inn is conveniently located near shops and restaurants.

Tips: Inquire about special deals during the off-peak season to save even more on your stay.

4. Villa Franca

Price Range: Around $65 - $95 per night

Location: Via Diomede 6, 80045 Pompei, Italy

Check-in/Check-out Hours: Check-in from 12 PM; check-out until 10 AM

Description: This charming villa features spacious rooms and a welcoming atmosphere. It's just a short walk from the archaeological park.

Tips: Enjoy the complimentary breakfast in the garden area to start your day off right.

5. Hotel Iside

Price Range: Approximately $60 - $85 per night

## ANTHONY BOLDS

Location: Via Minutella 27, 80045 Pompei, Italy

Check-in/Check-out Hours: Check-in from 2 PM; check-out until 11 AM

Description: Surrounded by citrus trees, this hotel offers a peaceful retreat with easy access to tourist attractions.

Tips: Utilize the free parking if you're traveling by car, and explore the nearby local markets.

ANTHONY BOLDS

# CHAPTER 11

## SHOPPING AND SOUVENIRS

## LOCAL MARKETS AND ARTISAN SHOPS

1. Mercato di Pompei

Location: Via Roma, Pompeii

Opening Hours: Monday to Saturday, 8:00 AM – 1:00 PM

Prices: Fresh produce starts at €1; specialty items up to €50

Tips: Arrive early to enjoy the freshest goods and a quieter shopping experience.

Description: This bustling market is the heartbeat of local commerce. Vendors offer a variety of fresh fruits, vegetables, cheeses, and meats. It's an ideal place to sample regional delicacies and observe daily life in Pompeii.

2. Artisan Ceramics Shop

Location: Via Plinio, Pompeii

**ANTHONY BOLDS**

Opening Hours: Daily, 9:00 AM – 7:00 PM

Prices: Handmade ceramics range from €10 to €200

Tips: Engage with artisans to learn about traditional crafting techniques.

Description: Specializing in pottery inspired by ancient designs, this shop showcases beautifully crafted ceramics. Each piece reflects the area's heritage, making it a perfect spot for unique souvenirs.

3. Limoncello Workshop

Location: Piazza Porta Marina Inferiore, Pompeii

Opening Hours: Monday to Sunday, 10:00 AM – 6:00 PM

Prices: Bottles priced between €15 and €40

Tips: Participate in a tasting session to find your favorite flavor.

Description: Discover the zesty flavor of authentic limoncello at this local producer. Learn about the distillation process and enjoy samples of this classic Italian liqueur.

4. Antique Bookstore

Location: Via Sacra, Pompeii

Opening Hours: Tuesday to Sunday, 10:00 AM – 5:00 PM

Prices: Vintage books and prints from €5 to €150

Tips: Explore the back sections for rare finds and historical texts.

Description: A haven for literature enthusiasts, this bookstore offers a wide array of antique books, maps, and prints related to Pompeii's history and broader Italian culture.

5. Leather Goods Boutique

Location: Corso Resina, Pompeii

Opening Hours: Monday to Saturday, 9:30 AM – 7:30 PM

Prices: Wallets from €25; jackets up to €300

Tips: Look for items made from locally sourced leather for superior quality.

**ANTHONY BOLDS**

Description: This boutique features high-quality leather products, including bags, belts, and jackets. Each item is crafted with meticulous attention to detail, embodying Italian craftsmanship.

6. Local Art Gallery

Location: Via Villa dei Misteri, Pompeii

Opening Hours: Daily, 10:00 AM – 6:00 PM

Prices: Art pieces starting at €50

Tips: Attend a workshop to create your own piece of art.

Description: Showcasing works by local artists, this gallery offers a glimpse into contemporary interpretations of Pompeii's legacy. It's an inspiring place to appreciate art influenced by the city's rich past.

7. Handcrafted Jewelry Store

Location: Via dell'Abbondanza, Pompeii

Opening Hours: Monday to Sunday, 10:00 AM – 8:00 PM

Prices: Pieces range from €20 to €250

Tips: Consider custom designs for a personalized memento.

Description: This store features exquisite jewelry inspired by ancient Roman designs. Each handcrafted piece is a testament to the artisans' skill and the region's artistic traditions.

## BUYING AUTHENTIC CRAFTS

### Understanding the importance of authentic crafts

Authentic Pompeii crafts are more than just souvenirs; they reflect centuries-old traditions that have been passed down through generations. These products encapsulate the soul of the historic city, allowing you to carry a piece of its history with you.

### Where to Find Genuine Crafts.

1. Local Markets: Take a stroll through the busy markets, where sellers sell homemade goods. Here, you'll find a wide range of things, from ceramics to fabrics, all carefully crafted.

2. Artisan Workshops: Visit workshops where artisans make their products on-site. Observing the crafting process gives insight into the talent and dedication required.

3. Authorized Shops: Buy from reputed stores that provide authentic products. Local authorities often certify or endorse these establishments.

## Crafts to Consider

1. Pottery and Ceramics: Pompeiian pottery is known for its beautiful designs and historical motifs, making it a timeless remembrance.

2. Mosaics: Inspired by ancient Roman art, these intricate works span from small coasters to enormous wall decorations.

3. Jewelry: Handmade jewelry with local stones or designs reminiscent of antiquity can be a treasured keepsake.

4. Fresco Replicas: Artists replicate historic frescoes discovered in Pompeii, giving you the opportunity to possess a piece of art history.

## Tips to Ensure Authenticity

1. Inquire about the Crafting Process: Talk to the seller about how and where the item was manufactured. Genuine craftspeople will happily tell their stories.

2. Look for Certificates: Some things come with a certificate of authenticity, particularly at authorized stores.

3. Be Wary of Pricing That Appears Too Good to Be True: Extremely low pricing may imply mass-produced rather than handcrafted goods.

## Supporting local artisans

Buying original crafts helps the local economy and promotes the preservation of traditional art forms. It's a great way to give back to the community while also getting a one-of-a-kind souvenir.

## ANTIQUE HUNTING

Antique hunting in Pompeii is a wonderful way to connect with the vestiges of ancient Roman life. Exploring markets and specialty shops yields things that tell stories about the past, ranging from antique pottery fragments to miniature figurines that evoke the creativity of the time. For anybody interested in history and relics, exploring these areas may be an adventure in discovering hidden gems that have stood the test of time.

Local sellers and antique dealers frequently trade in Roman-style antiquities. While most artifacts are copies, created to accurately mimic old patterns, they nonetheless offer the opportunity to own a piece of artistry from the past. It is critical to work with competent dealers who can explain the historical significance and authenticity of each item. There's a lot to learn about coins, jewelry influenced by Roman patterns, and tools similar to those used in ancient workshops.

Antique shops in Pompeii provide wonderfully restored furniture and ornamental objects that preserve the essence of Roman interior design. Some pieces, while not old, are made with techniques and materials that are historically accurate, allowing visitors to bring a little of Pompeii into their homes. Exploring these businesses may be an interesting experience, providing insight into how Romans lived and decorated their homes.

Collectors and individuals with an eye for rare treasures should learn about Italian antiquities sales and export rules. Understanding these rules ensures that purchases are lawful and respectful of Italy's cultural heritage. With adequate research and supervision, the joy of discovering an item with historical significance becomes a gratifying quest.

A visit to the local flea markets in and around Pompeii yields a variety of antique-inspired items. These markets are vivid and active, displaying not just products relating to Roman antiquity, but also vintage treasures from many periods of Italian history. By interacting with the merchants, visitors may learn about the tales behind each object, making each purchase meaningful and profoundly connected to history.

## TIPS ON BARGAINING AND SHOPPING ETIQUETTE

1. Understand the local culture.

In Italy, most stores have fixed prices, and haggling is not customary. However, in open-air marketplaces or with street vendors, there may be room for negotiation. It is critical to approach bargaining with consideration for local customs.

2. Learn some basic Italian phrases.

Knowing a few easy phrases can go a long way toward developing rapport with merchants. Phrases such as "How much does this cost?" ( "Quanto costa?" ) such as "Can you offer a better price?" Using phrases like "Può farmi un prezzo migliore?" can enhance interactions and improve the overall experience.

3. Be polite and friendly.

A friendly hello and a smile can set the tone for your interaction. Italians value courtesy, thus beginning with "Good day" ("Buongiorno") can make a difference.

4. Show genuine interest.

Demonstrating genuine appreciation for an item might often persuade the vendor to provide a discount. Ask inquiries about the goods to demonstrate curiosity while still respecting the seller's knowledge.

5. Avoid Aggressive haggling.

While some negotiating is permissible in certain situations, pushing too far might be perceived as rude. If a seller denies your offer, you should accept their price or politely go on.

6. Have cash ready.

Smaller sellers can prefer cash transactions. Carrying little dollars and coins might make shopping easier and may even help you negotiate a modest discount.

7. Be aware of counterfeits.

Keep a watch out for imitations. Authenticity is appreciated, and buying real local crafts benefits the community.

8. Respect the merchandise.

Handle anything with caution and seek permission if you are unsure whether touching is permitted. Treating products with care demonstrates respect for the seller's property.

9. Know when to walk away.

If the price is not within your budget, it is okay to gently thank the merchant and depart. This can sometimes result in a better offer but don't anticipate it.

# CHAPTER 12

## PRACTICAL INFORMATION

## CURRENCY EXCHANGE AND BANKING

Currency exchange and banking are important factors to consider while arranging a trip to Pompeii. Navigating the local financial system with ease guarantees a seamless and joyful encounter. Italy uses the euro (€), so having some cash on hand can be useful, especially for modest purchases like souvenirs, snacks, or local transportation. While most places accept major credit and debit cards, cash is still frequently utilized in rural towns and markets.

To get the greatest conversion rate, avoid currency exchange kiosks at airports or tourist destinations, as they typically charge greater fees and give less favorable rates. Instead, use local banks or ATMs, which typically offer a better rate and cheaper fees.

Banks in Pompeii are normally open from the morning until early afternoon, closing for a few hours before returning later in the afternoon. Be aware of these hours and schedule your banking requirements appropriately.

ATMs are readily available in and around Pompeii for cash withdrawals, and using your bank card to get euros is a convenient option. Before you travel, check with your bank to see if there are any international transaction fees or withdrawal limits. Inform your bank about your travel plans to avoid card issues or blockages.

Some banks and foreign exchange firms provide prepaid travel cards, which can be a secure way to manage your money. These cards allow you to load funds in euros, making transactions easier and eliminating the need for cash.

Opening a temporary bank account in Italy may be an option for visitors who want to stay for an extended period of time, while it is normally more practical for longer stays. English-speaking employees are frequently accessible in big banks, making it easier for visitors who are not fluent in Italian.

Pompeii's proximity to Naples allows you to access a wide range of financial services, including international banks with branches or partners in the area. These services may help with currency exchange, overseas transfers, and other banking needs besides simple withdrawals.

## COMMUNICATION: SIM CARDS AND WI-FI ACCESS

It is simple and convenient to stay connected when visiting Pompeii. Knowing how to use SIM cards and Wi-Fi in the area might improve your trip, whether you need to use them for local calls, map navigation, or social media.

SIM cards are widely accessible in telecom shops, convenience stores, and airports. Travelers can choose from a variety of reasonably priced prepaid SIM alternatives from Italian mobile companies like TIM, Vodafone, and WindTre. These packages frequently come with texting features, international phone minutes, and significant data allotments. Make sure your phone is unlocked before buying a SIM card, and bring a legitimate ID because registration is necessary. After everything is set up, you may use the provider's app or website to control your balance and data consumption.

Pompeii has a number of choices for visitors who would rather stay connected via Wi-Fi. You may stay online while eating or drinking coffee at a lot of cafés, restaurants, and hotels that offer free Wi-Fi. Portable Wi-Fi hotspots can be purchased online in advance of your trip or rented from vendors in large cities if you would rather have a more reliable connection while touring. These devices are a great choice for families or groups because they offer dependable internet access while on the go and can support several users simultaneously.

Some locations near Pompeii, including the archeological site, also have public Wi-Fi, however, it might not be as dependable as connections provided by businesses. For a more seamless experience, it is advised to have a backup plan, such as a SIM card with mobile data, particularly when using navigation or translation apps while you are there.

# EMERGENCY CONTACTS AND MEDICAL FACILITIES

Italy's emergency services can be reached via a few key phone numbers. If you require immediate medical attention, phone 118 to contact the medical emergency service, which can dispatch ambulances and provide rapid aid. For police assistance, dial 113; for fire situations, dial 115. Having these numbers readily available allows a prompt reaction if an unexpected crisis develops.

Pompeii has various pharmacies throughout the town where visitors can buy over-the-counter drugs and get advice from qualified pharmacists. Pharmacies are generally marked with a green cross, making them easily identifiable. Most pharmacists speak English and can help with mild diseases like headaches, colds, or intestinal problems. It is advisable to bring a small first-aid kit for basic needs, but knowing the locations of these pharmacies can be useful for more specific health issues.

Several hospitals and clinics are nearby for those who require more serious medical assistance. The nearest large hospital is in Torre Annunziata, which is only a short drive from Pompeii. This facility is outfitted with emergency services, general care, and specialty departments. Private clinics provide a variety of medical services, including consultations and minor treatments, with lower wait periods. Having travel insurance that covers overseas medical bills is recommended since it makes it easier to acquire private healthcare services.

Another important step is to find the tourist information centers in Pompeii. These centers provide emergency aid, including language translation and instructions to the nearest medical institutions. The staff is usually prepared to answer frequent traveler questions and may connect you with relevant resources if you have any problems.

Staying prepared not only assures a safer experience but also allows you to explore with greater confidence, knowing that assistance is accessible if necessary. Remember to carry a list of emergency contacts with you, including your home country's embassy or consulate in

Italy, which can be a vital resource in the event of a serious issue.

## LEGAL MATTERS AND TRAVELER RIGHTS

Travelers must respect the archaeological site's integrity. Touching, climbing on ruins, and removing antiquities are highly prohibited and may result in serious penalties or legal action. Pompeii is a protected cultural heritage site, and the Italian government takes stringent precautions to preserve its past. Adhering to these regulations preserves Pompeii's legacy for future generations.

It's also worth noting that photography is often allowed in Pompeii. However, permissions for business purposes, such as the use of tripods or professional equipment, must be secured ahead of time. Using drones without authority is not permitted on the archaeological site. Before organizing a visit, travelers should check for updates or changes in regulations.

If you run into problems, such as conflicts with vendors or unanticipated legal challenges, keep in mind that you have some rights as a guest. Italy has consumer protection regulations that protect travelers from unfair treatment. If the quality of service does not reach the promised standards, you have the right to submit a complaint to the local authorities or seek aid from tourist offices.

Medical emergencies are another factor to consider when traveling. The Italian healthcare system provides services to travelers, although it is recommended that they carry travel insurance that covers medical expenses. European Union citizens can use their European Health Insurance Card (EHIC) to obtain medical services, while non-EU tourists must have proper coverage. Emergency lines are available in case of an emergency, and passengers should become acquainted with them for their own protection.

Being aware of local regulations applies to transportation as well. When hiring a car, tourists must carry both their international driver's license and a valid driver's license from their home country. It is critical to follow traffic laws, such as wearing seatbelts and driving within speed limits. Violations can result in fines, which, if not paid, can jeopardize future travel plans within Italy.

Preserving your personal things and understanding your rights in the event of theft is critical. If something is stolen, you must immediately report the event to the local police. You will need to make a report for insurance claims or if you require replacement documents, such as passports. Many sections of Pompeii are secure, however, caution is always advised, especially in busier areas where pickpocketing can occur.

## TRAVEL INSURANCE CONSIDERATIONS

Before acquiring a travel insurance plan, you should determine what coverage is best for your needs. Standard travel insurance usually includes medical coverage, trip cancellation protection, and assistance with misplaced or delayed luggage. Medical coverage is extremely important when traveling abroad. In the event of illness or injury, insurance helps cover medical bills such as hospital stays or emergency transports, which would otherwise be costly for travelers.

Another important consideration is travel cancellation or interruption coverage. This protects you from unanticipated events like flight cancellations, personal emergencies, or unexpected health difficulties that may compel you to adjust your vacation arrangements. With this in place, you are more likely to obtain compensation for non-refundable charges, which protects your financial investment in the trip.

Accident and emergency evacuation insurance is also recommended. Visiting historic sites frequently entails walking on rough terrain, and such insurance provides access to vital medical attention and transportation in the event of an accident. Evacuation insurance ensures that you will receive competent medical assistance regardless of where you are exploring.

It is also advisable to get coverage that covers lost or delayed luggage. Arriving at your destination without your possessions is frustrating, but having coverage means you may recover money for important items. This is especially important if your luggage becomes delayed or misplaced during international travel.

**ANTHONY BOLDS**

When choosing travel insurance, it's important to study the policy information attentively. Some policies may include exclusions or limitations based on pre-existing conditions or specified behaviors, so it's important to understand what is and isn't covered. Comparing several providers and their products might help you discover a plan that meets your budget and travel needs.

# CHAPTER 13

## TRAVELER'S TIPS

## PACKING ESSENTIALS FOR EVERY SEASON

Spring temperatures are pleasant, although unexpected rain showers are prevalent. Pack a lightweight, water-resistant jacket, as well as appropriate walking shoes for cobblestone streets. Layers are your friend this season; choose breathable long-sleeve shirts and sweaters that can be easily added and withdrawn. Sunglasses and a hat are useful for protecting your eyes from the sun while exploring archeological sites.

Summer in Pompeii is quite hot, therefore light, airy attire is needed. Cotton and linen materials let you stay cool while exploring the ancient sites. A wide-brimmed hat and high-SPF sunscreen will shield you from the sun's rays. Hydration is essential, so bringing a reusable water bottle is a sensible option. Comfortable sandals or sneakers with a high grip are also essential for crossing uneven ground safely.

As autumn approaches, temperatures begin to decrease, particularly at night. A lightweight jacket or sweater is ideal for layering over daytime attire. Pack long-sleeved shirts, comfortable slacks, and a scarf to keep warm on breezy nights. Rain may fall, so packing an umbrella or small raincoat is a good idea.

Winter in Pompeii is normally milder than in other regions of Europe, but it can still be cold, especially in the mornings and at night. Medium-weight coats, thick sweaters, and long leggings are suitable. Gloves and a scarf may also come in helpful, particularly if you intend to visit outdoor attractions early in the day. Waterproof footwear will keep your feet dry in wet conditions.

## CULTURAL DO'S AND DON'TS

### Respect the Archaeological Sites

Pompeii is not just a tourist destination; it's a UNESCO World Heritage site with immense historical value. Respect the ruins by staying on marked paths, avoiding touching or climbing on ancient structures, and refraining from taking anything from the site. Photography is usually allowed, but it's important to be mindful of any specific rules regarding flash or tripods.

### Dress Modestly in Religious Sites

If you plan to visit churches or other religious landmarks around Pompeii, modest clothing is advised. This often means covering shoulders and knees. Bringing a light shawl or scarf can be convenient, as it allows you to quickly adapt if needed.

### Use Polite Gestures and Greetings

When interacting with locals, polite greetings are appreciated. A simple "Buongiorno" (Good morning) or "Buonasera" (Good evening) goes a long way. Italians value respectful conversation, so practicing a few basic Italian phrases can make interactions more pleasant and show genuine interest.

## Dining Etiquette Matters

When dining in local restaurants or cafés, be aware of dining customs. Italians take their meals seriously, and meals are seen as a time to relax and enjoy. Avoid rushing through your food, and remember that it's courteous to greet the staff upon entering and say "Grazie" (Thank you) when leaving. If tipping, it's usually a small gesture, as service charges are often included in the bill.

## Be Mindful of Public Behavior

Public spaces, especially in historic sites like Pompeii, are areas where respect is crucial. Loud conversations, disruptive behavior, or littering can be seen as disrespectful. Keeping noise levels down and disposing of trash properly shows regard for both the environment and the people around you.

ANTHONY BOLDS

## Appreciate Local Customs without Stereotyping

Pompeii and its surrounding areas have rich traditions that may differ from what you're accustomed to. Show interest and appreciation without imposing your expectations. For example, Italians might have a different sense of time when it comes to opening hours or meal times, so patience is valued. Embrace these differences with a positive attitude.

## Avoid Excessive PDA (Public Displays of Affection)

While affectionate gestures are common in Italian culture, excessive displays in historic or religious areas may not be appropriate. Keep physical affection discreet when visiting such locations to maintain a respectful atmosphere.

## Observe Proper Conduct in Museums and Exhibitions

Pompeii offers numerous opportunities to explore artifacts and exhibitions. When visiting these areas, refrain from touching displays, and follow the guidelines posted for each exhibit. These artifacts are invaluable, and it's essential to help preserve them for future generations.

## Respect Local Transportation Etiquette

When using public transportation, such as buses or trains around Pompeii, give up seats for elderly passengers when needed. It's also courteous to allow people to exit before boarding. Being mindful of your volume during the ride shows respect for others who may be using this time to relax.

## Follow Guidelines During Festivities and Events

Pompeii hosts a variety of cultural events throughout the year, where local traditions are celebrated. When attending these, respect local customs and traditions, participate with enthusiasm, and avoid actions that might be seen as mocking or insensitive.

# STAYING SAFE: COMMON SCAMS AND HOW TO AVOID THEM

A frequent fraud involves unofficial guides who offer their services at the gate. These individuals may pretend to be certified and competent, but they frequently lack credentials and offer substandard services at exorbitant fees. To avoid this, always book your tours through reliable firms or at authorized ticket kiosks. Official guides wear identification and are immediately identifiable, ensuring that you receive accurate and useful information throughout your tour.

Another common ploy is the 'overpriced memento' trap. Vendors may approach things purporting to be real or unique to Pompeii, however, they are frequently mass-produced and sold at inflated costs. It's a good idea to investigate local shops ahead of time or to stick to established marketplaces where prices are more stable and there is room for acceptable negotiating.

Taxis and transportation services may occasionally overpay or take longer routes to increase charges. To avoid this, always utilize regulated taxi services or ridesharing applications with predetermined fares and controlled routes. If you take a cab, confirm the fare before you begin your journey, and keep an eye on the GPS to ensure a direct path.

Another thing to keep an eye out for is bogus 'friendly locals' who offer to aid with ticket sales or instructions. They frequently direct tourists to more expensive services or request a tip for their 'help.' Politely decline these offers and consult official signage, maps, or staff for assistance.

Credit card skimming is a concern in every tourist-heavy area. When making a purchase, be wary about handing up your card. Choose secure payment methods, such as contactless payments, and keep your card in sight at all times. If you prefer cash, withdraw money only from ATMs located within banks or in highly visible areas to decrease the possibility of tampered machines.

Being aware of common parking scams is also vital. Unauthorized attendants may charge a fee to watch your vehicle. Official parking locations will have well-indicated signs and payment devices. Use these services to safeguard the safety of your vehicle and avoid unwanted expenses.

## HEALTH TIPS: STAYING WELL ABROAD

Maintaining good health when visiting Pompeii can improve the trip and guarantee uninterrupted, unforgettable experiences. Before the trip, preparation begins. To discuss any required drugs and to check on vaccines, it is advisable to make an appointment with a healthcare professional. A compact first-aid kit with basic supplies including bandages, painkillers, antiseptic wipes, and any necessary prescription medications should be brought by travelers. This planning facilitates the timely resolution of minor health conditions.

Staying hydrated is essential while visiting outdoor locations like Pompeii. Dehydration can be avoided by carrying a reusable water bottle and drinking it throughout the day, particularly in the warmer months. Since water quality varies, it is usually safer to stick to bottled or filtered water.

Sun protection is also crucial. Using sunglasses, hats, and sunscreen with a high SPF protects the skin and eyes against strong sunshine. Clothing that is breathable and lightweight can give both comfort and sun protection. Avoiding the hottest parts of the day can be achieved by exploring in the early morning or late afternoon.

Maintaining energy levels when traveling requires eating healthily. Savoring regional food is a highlight, but it's crucial to pick meals from reliable restaurants that are fresh and cooked to perfection. The risk of stomach problems might be decreased by avoiding street foods that might not have been properly prepared or kept. When handwashing stations may not be available, it is useful to have hand sanitizer on hand to use prior to meals.

Another strategy to stay motivated is to continue being physically active. Although exploring archeological sites is a great way to get exercise, it's important to wear comfortable shoes to avoid weariness and blisters. The body and mind are kept invigorated by taking breaks, resting, and allowing time to recuperate in between tasks.

A safe experience is guaranteed by paying attention to your surroundings and heeding safety instructions. It's wise to keep up with local health regulations and be aware of where to get medical help if necessary. Having a list of emergency contacts, such as nearby medical centers and embassies, is a preventative measure that offers comfort.

## SOLO TRAVEL ADVICE

First, it's crucial to organize your trip ahead of time. Find out when the archeological sites are open, and think about buying your admission tickets online. You may avoid the crowds and save time by doing this. The ability to explore at their own leisure is something that solo travelers frequently value, and scheduling some activities in advance, like guided tours, can help you gain a deeper grasp of Pompeii's past without feeling overburdened.

Priority should be given to safety, particularly when traveling alone. It's important to keep your belongings safe, so choose a tiny backpack or crossbody bag with tight-fitting zippers. Although Pompeii is typically safe, it's a good idea to be on your guard, especially in crowded locations or when taking public transit. Just in case, make sure you have the phone numbers of emergency services and local authorities stored on your device.

When done on your own, exploring Pompeii may be an exciting experience. In the vast archeological site, a decent map or a trustworthy offline navigation tool can be really helpful. From the old villas to the restored frescoes, exploring alone gives you greater freedom in choosing which locations to see first. It's an opportunity to stop and take in the information that most appeals to you.

Some people find eating by themselves to be difficult while traveling alone, but in Pompeii, it's a wonderful experience. Solo travelers can savor delectable Italian food at local trattorias and cafes without having to hustle. It's also a chance to talk to locals, find out about their favorite foods, and gain more knowledge about the region. Eating meals outside during the day or early evening is frequently a cozy approach to take in the surroundings and feel a part of the community.

Solo travelers have a variety of lodging options, ranging from boutique hotels to affordable hostels. Choose lodgings that are conveniently situated so that you may easily access the ruins and local transit. It might be enjoyable and helpful to stay somewhere where you can meet other tourists. You can make new friends, exchange advice, or even locate day trip partners.

Solo travel gives you more freedom if you want to spend more time than just Pompeii. Day trips to neighboring locations like Sorrento, Capri, or the Amalfi Coast are simple and allow you to explore at your own speed. Because ferry and train services sometimes change, it is advised to check transit timetables ahead of time. It can be useful to know some basic Italian phrases, particularly when asking for directions or navigating these routes.

# CHAPTER 14

## RESOURCES AND FURTHER READING

## USEFUL WEBSITES AND APPS

1. Essential Websites

Official Pompeii Archaeological Park Website

The official site provides up-to-date information on opening hours, ticket prices, and any special events taking place within the archaeological park. It also offers insights into the current exhibitions and visitor facilities. It's a reliable source for planning your visit and ensuring you have all the necessary details before you arrive.

**Campania Tourism Portal**

This regional tourism website offers a comprehensive guide to not only Pompeii but also the surrounding areas, such as Naples and the Amalfi Coast. It includes tips on accommodation, dining, and transportation options, making it a one-stop resource for trip planning. Whether you're looking for the best routes to Pompeii or nearby attractions, this site has you covered.

ANTHONY BOLDS

## UNESCO World Heritage Site Listing for Pompeii

The UNESCO page provides a deeper historical and cultural context for Pompeii, highlighting its global significance. It's an excellent resource for those wanting to learn more about why Pompeii is considered an essential part of world heritage, enhancing your appreciation of the ruins during your visit.

2. Must-Have Apps

## MyPompeii

This app acts as a personal guide, offering maps and audio tours that sync with your location as you explore the ruins. It provides details about each site you visit, from temples and villas to frescoes and mosaics, enriching your understanding of the historical context. The app also includes suggested walking routes based on your interests, ensuring a tailored experience.

## Trainline

For those traveling from Naples or other nearby cities, Trainline is invaluable. It offers real-time updates on train schedules, ticket prices, and platform information, helping you reach Pompeii efficiently. You can book tickets directly through the app, saving time and avoiding long queues at the station.

**Google Maps**

While simple, Google Maps remains a powerful tool for navigating both the archaeological site and the modern town of Pompeii. It provides step-by-step directions, reviews of nearby restaurants and cafés, and walking paths within the ruins. It's a helpful resource for staying on track and finding your way around effortlessly.

**Pompeii Self-Guided Tour App**

This app offers a self-paced experience, providing you with information and stories about each point of interest. It's perfect for those who prefer to explore at their own pace while still gaining insights from a knowledgeable source. The offline feature is especially useful, as it allows you to access content without relying on Wi-Fi or data.

## TripAdvisor

TripAdvisor's app is a fantastic resource for discovering the best local experiences, including guided tours, restaurants, and accommodations in Pompeii. The platform's extensive collection of user reviews offers insights from fellow travelers, helping you choose the most recommended services. You can also book tours and tickets directly, making trip planning seamless.

3. Connectivity and Language Assistance

## Google Translate

Language barriers can sometimes be challenging, especially when visiting a foreign country. Google Translate helps bridge that gap by translating signs, menus, and even conversations instantly. The app's offline mode ensures you have language support even when you don't have internet access, making interactions with locals easier.

## Wi-Fi Finder

For travelers needing reliable internet access, Wi-Fi Finder identifies hotspots around Pompeii. It provides directions to nearby cafes, libraries, and other establishments where you can connect for free or for a small fee. Staying connected helps you access other digital tools and keep your travel plans on track.

## XE Currency Converter

This app is ideal for managing currency exchanges, particularly if you're visiting from outside the Eurozone. XE offers real-time conversion rates, ensuring you understand the cost of souvenirs, meals, and other expenses without confusion. The app works offline as well, making it a dependable travel companion.

# LOCAL TOURIST OFFICES AND INFORMATION CENTERS

1. Pompeii Visitor Information Center

Description: Located near the main entrance of the archaeological site, this center provides comprehensive information about the ruins, nearby attractions, and current events. Knowledgeable staff are on hand to answer questions and assist with planning your itinerary.

Location: Piazza Esedra, 80045 Pompeii NA, Italy

Phone Number: +39 081 857 5347

Tips: Stop by to pick up a detailed map and learn about guided tour options. The staff can also inform you about any special exhibitions or changes in opening hours.

2. Pompeii Tourism Office

Description: Situated in the heart of the town, this office offers information on local accommodations, dining options, and transportation. They can help with bookings and provide insights into lesser-known sites in the area.

**ANTHONY BOLDS**

Location: Via Sacra, 1, 80045 Pompeii NA, Italy

Phone Number: +39 081 850 7255

Tips: Visit this office if you're interested in exploring beyond the archaeological site, such as trips to Mount Vesuvius or the Amalfi Coast.

3. Information Point inside Pompeii Ruins

Description: Found within the archaeological park, this information point assists visitors already inside the ruins. Staff can help with navigation and offer historical context for the various structures you encounter.

Location: Inside Pompeii Archaeological Park, near the Forum

Phone Number: +39 081 857 5111

Tips: If you have questions during your exploration, this is the place to get quick answers and enhance your understanding of the site's significance.

## Helpful Tips for Your Visit

1. Language Support: Staff members typically speak multiple languages, including English, to assist international travelers.

2. Operating Hours: Most tourist offices are open from 8:30 AM to 7:30 PM. It's wise to confirm the hours before your visit, especially on holidays.

3. Accessibility Information: These centers can provide details on accessible routes and facilities for visitors with mobility needs.

## CONCLUSION

By the end of this comprehensive tour, you will have gained a wealth of knowledge about Pompeii, one of the world's most compelling sites. This historic city, which was buried for ages under volcanic ash, now stands as an extraordinary window into the past. Throughout the walk, we traveled together among its historic ruins, learned about the secrets engraved into the frescoes and mosaics, and discovered the daily lives of Roman inhabitants whose legacies can still be heard in every corner.

You've thoroughly visited the archeological park, which has rich layers of history exposed through expert-guided tours and immersive virtual reality activities that bring ancient Pompeii to life. From the towering Temple of Apollo to the delicate features of Roman architecture, you've witnessed how this city functions as a living museum for people seeking information and adventure.

We ventured beyond the ruins to explore the region's colorful culture. We discovered the finest ways to surrounding gems such as Herculaneum, Stabiae, and

Oplontis, each of which tells a unique story of the Roman Empire. With suggested walking paths, you may easily tour these ancient landscapes.

We also walked you through culinary marvels, from street cuisine to luxury dining experiences. With recommendations for great restaurants and cafés, street food tips, and vineyard excursions, you'll be ready to experience the authentic flavors of Campania.

This list covers everything from luxury hotels to mid-range accommodations, ensuring that your stay suits your interests and needs. For those eager for excitement, we presented information about Mount Vesuvius trips, including the best trails, suggestions, and rates for an unforgettable ascent.

Beyond the logistics, we've also covered the practical aspects of travel, such as emergency contacts and medical facilities, currency conversion, communication choices, and local customs. With this information, you can confidently and safely navigate Pompeii and its surroundings.

Now that you have all of this knowledge, it's time to make your ambitions a reality. Pompeii is more than simply an ancient site; it's an experience waiting to happen, providing the ideal blend of history, culture, and adventure for every visitor. Whether you're attracted by its ruins, eager to sample its tastes, or keen to discover hidden routes, this adventure will make an indelible impression on your spirit.

Take the next step: purchase your tickets, arrange your schedule, and immerse yourself in a timeless trip that reconnects you with the past while generating amazing memories. Pompeii awaits, and the stories you write there will be yours to keep for a lifetime. So, why wait? Your Roman trip is only a decision away.

Start your Pompeii journey today.

Printed in Dunstable, United Kingdom